THE OFFICIAL ROBOT GUIDE

PENGUIN BOOKS

Penguin Books

Published by the Penguin Group
Penguin Books Ltd, 27 Wrights Lane,
London W8 5TZ, England
Penguin Putnam Inc., 375 Hudson Street,
New York, New York 10014, USA
Penguin Books Australia Ltd, Ringwood,
Victoria, Australia
Penguin Books Canada Ltd, 10 Alcorn Avenue, Toronto, Ontario, Canada M4V 3B2
Penguin Books India (P) Ltd, 11 Community Centre, Panchsheel Park, New Delhi – 110 017, India
Penguin Books (NZ) Ltd, Cnr Rosedale and Airborne Roads, Albany, Auckland, New Zealand
Penguin Books (South Africa) (Pty) Ltd,
5 Watkins Street, Denver Ext 4,
Johannesburg 2094, South Africa

On the World Wide Web at: www.penguin.com

Penguin Books Ltd, Registered Offices: Harmondsworth, Middlesex, England

First published 2001
4

Set in Bank Gothic

Made and printed in England by Butler & Tanner Ltd

British Library Cataloguing in Publication Data
A CIP catalogue record for this book is available from the British Library

ISBN 0-141-31319-6

Contents

INTRODUCTION

Robot Wars – the most exciting, the most violent and the most unpredictable show on television today. You've experienced the thrills, the carnage, the highs and the lows. But how much do you know about the Robots? Did you know that Chaos 2 was built from two lawnmower engines or that Velocirippa's self-righting device makes it untoppable? How about the fact that the hideous Banshee took less than five weeks to build and appeared as Shark Attack in series three? Packed with fascinating facts and figures, you can learn from this book everything there is to know about the competitors and house robots that appeared in the Fourth Great War

Over 300 robots were auditioned. Only sixty-four of the most audacious made it on to the small screen along with thirty-two seeded entrants who had excelled in the previous series. They were all tested to the limit of their technical prowess, strength, speed and daring during the Fourth Great War and they're all pictured here before the batterings they received during the battles.

The six awesome, but by no means indestructible, house robots – Ref Bot, Shunt, Sir Killalot, Sergeant Bash, Dead Metal and the lovely Matilda – also feature in all their metallic glory.

As well as details about all the robots, we explain the rules of engagement from the heats to the Grand Final, from the Pinball Warrior Tournament to the Sumo Basho Competition.

Whether you're a successful or budding roboteer, or just love the carnage that is *Robot Wars*, this is the book for you.

The Fourth War

Total number of shows = 19
(16 heats, 2 semi-finals, 1 grand final)
Number of competitors per heat = 6 robots
Total number of competitors = 96 robots

The Heats

Round One

In Round One there are two melees each featuring three robots. In each battle, one robot is eliminated and the two remaining robots go through to Round Two.

Round Two

In Round Two the four remaining robots go head-to-head. Each robot battles against a winner from the other melee to avoid fighting the same robot twice. The two winners go through to Round Three.

Round Three

The two robots meet in a head-to-head. The winner goes on to battle in the Series' semi-finals.

Round 1	Round 2	Round 3	Heat Winner
Robot	Robot		
Robot		Robot	
Robot	Robot		
			Robot
Robot	Robot		
Robot		Robot	
Robot	Robot		

The Semi-Finals

Number of heat winners = 16
Total number of battles per semi-final = 6
(8 robots per show)

Round One

In Round One the eight robots meet in four head-to-head battles in a knockout format. The four winners then go on to Round Two.

Round Two

The four remaining robots go head-to-head once more, leaving two overall winners. Both these winners go through to the Grand Final. As there are two semi-final shows four robots will compete in the Grand Final.

Round 1	Round 2	Semi-Final Winners
Robot		
	Robot	
Robot		
		Robot
Robot		
	Robot	
Robot		
Robot		
	Robot	
Robot		
		Robot
Robot		
	Robot	
Robot		

The Grand Final

Total number of battles
in the Grand Final = 4

Round One
In the Grand Final there are two Round One battles with two robots facing each other head-to-head.

Playoff
The two losing robots meet in a playoff battle to determine third and fourth place.

Grand Final
The two winners from Round One meet in the Grand Final battle to determine who will be the Robot Wars Grand Champion.

ROUND 1	GRAND FINAL	WINNER
Robot		
	Robot	
Robot		
		Robot Grand Champion
Robot		
	Robot	
Robot		
	PLAYOFF	
	Robot	
		Robot 3rd Place
	Robot	

Additional Events

Pinball

The 'Pinball Warrior Tournament' is the ultimate test of driver skill and ability. On each show individual robots attempt to score as many points as possible by attacking special targets and completing challenges around the arena whilst attempting to out-manoeuvre the house robots. Scores vary depending on the difficulty of dangers faced. Each game of Pinball takes place against the clock and whoever scores the most points within the allotted time will be declared the 'Pinball Warrior Champion'.

Sumo

The 'Sumo Basho' is a test of strength. The competitor robots have to try and push the House robot 'Shunt' out of the Sumo ring as quickly as possible. The scoring is based on the amount of time each competitor remains in the ring or how quickly they manage to dispatch Shunt from the ring.

House Robots

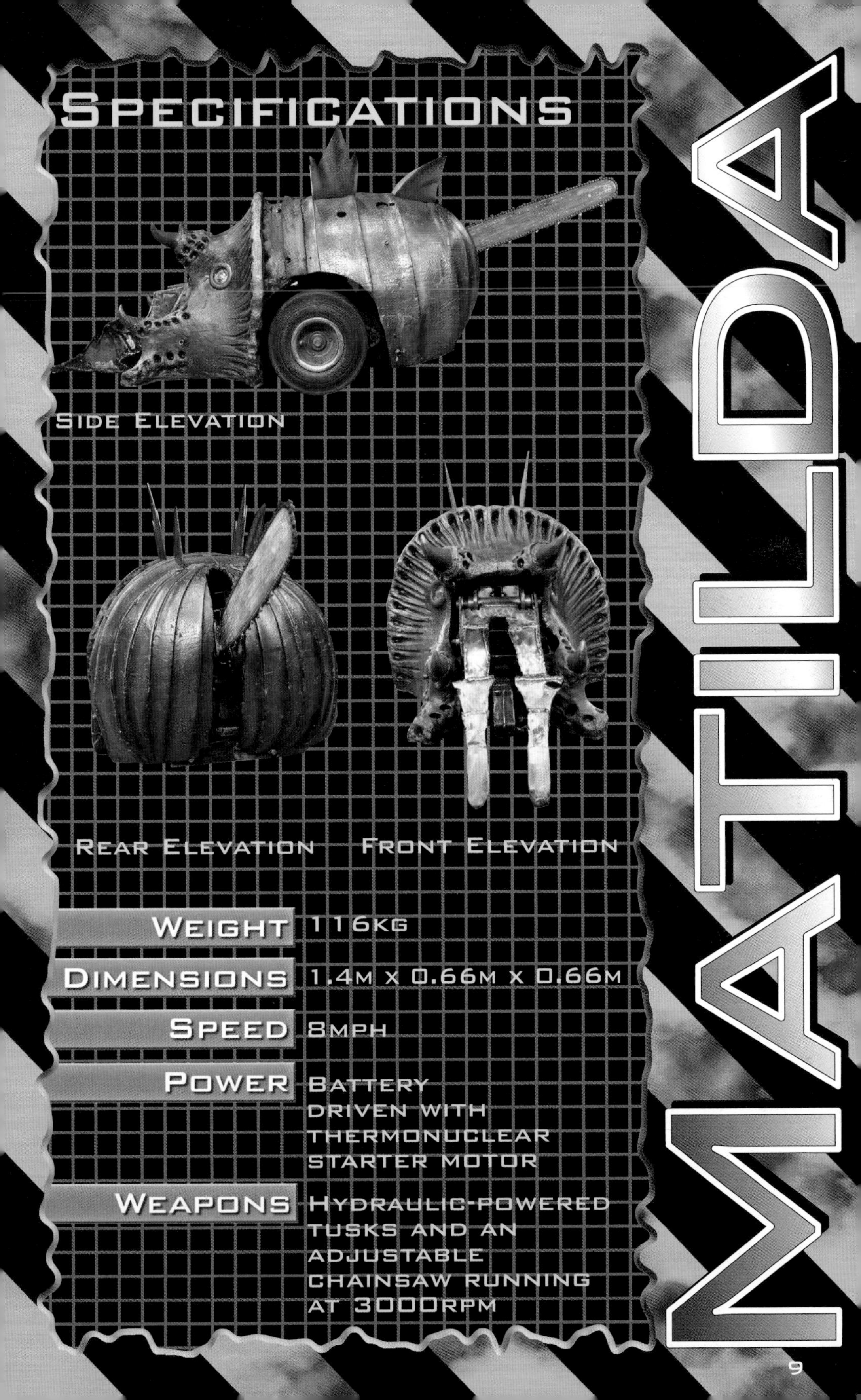
MATILDA
SPECIFICATIONS
SIDE ELEVATION
REAR ELEVATION
FRONT ELEVATION
WEIGHT 116KG
DIMENSIONS 1.4M X 0.66M X 0.66M
SPEED 8MPH
POWER BATTERY DRIVEN WITH THERMONUCLEAR STARTER MOTOR
WEAPONS HYDRAULIC-POWERED TUSKS AND AN ADJUSTABLE CHAINSAW RUNNING AT 3000RPM
9

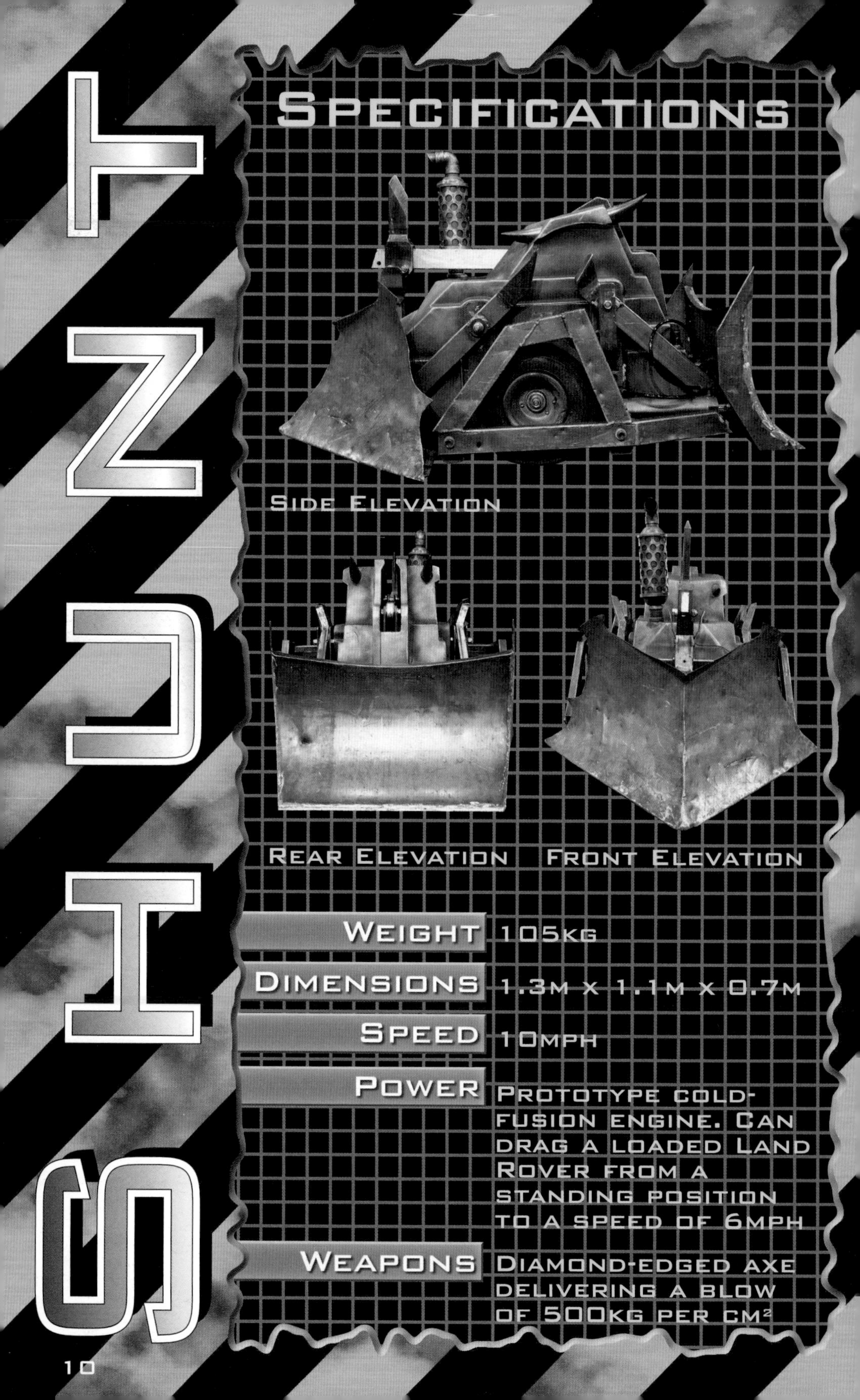
SHUNT
Specifications
Side Elevation
Rear Elevation
Front Elevation
Weight
105kg
Dimensions
1.3m x 1.1m x 0.7m
Speed
10mph
Power
Prototype cold-fusion engine. Can drag a loaded Land Rover from a standing position to a speed of 6mph
Weapons
Diamond-edged axe delivering a blow of 500kg per cm²

Sgt.
Bash.

SGT BASH
SPECIFICATIONS
SIDE ELEVATION
REAR ELEVATION
FRONT ELEVATION
WEIGHT 120KG
DIMENSIONS 1.4M X 0.9M X 0.9M
SPEED 8MPH
POWER FOUR BATTERIES RUNNING IN PARALLEL. CONDUITS ATTACHED TO FLAME THROWER VENT HEAT TO POWER STEAM ENGINE
WEAPONS PROPANE-FUELLED FLAME THROWER ON 360° TURRET. FRONT-MOUNTED PINCERS

SIR KILLALOT

SPECIFICATIONS

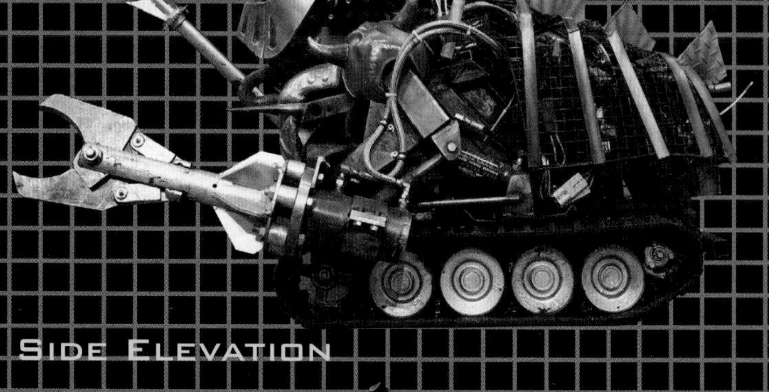

SIDE ELEVATION

REAR ELEVATION

FRONT ELEVATION

WEIGHT	280KG
DIMENSIONS	1.2M X 1.2M X 1.3M
SPEED	5MPH
POWER	PETROL-DRIVEN ENGINE WITH HYDRAULIC POWER PACKS
WEAPONS	HYDRAULIC LANCE AND CUTTER

DEAD METAL

Specifications

Side Elevation

Rear Elevation

Front Elevation

Weight	112kg
Dimensions	1.6m x 1m x 0.7m
Speed	12mph
Power	Battery-driven engine with thermonuclear starter motor
Weapons	Pneumatic pincers and an adjustable 3000rpm circular saw

REFBOT

Specifications

Side Elevation

Rear Elevation

Front Elevation

Weight	120kg
Dimensions	1.4m x 0.9m x 1.3m
Speed	7mph
Power	Battery powered

Seeds

The Robot Wars Steering Committee, composed of roboteers, production team and our technical experts, compiled a list of Seeds based on previous experience, performance, innovation and creativity. These seeded competitors gain automatic entry to the fourth wars.

1 Chaos 2
2 Hypno-Disc
3 Razer
4 Panic Attack II
5 Fire Storm II
6 Behemoth
7 Steg 2
8 Gemini
9 101
10 Spawn of Scutter
11 Wild Thing
12 Evil Weevil
13 Gravedigger
14 Bigger Brother
15 Wheely Big Cheese
16 Killerhurtz
17 King B3
18 Cerberus
19 Pussycat
20 Aggrobot II
21 Diótóir
22 X-terminator II
23 Mortis
24 Berserk 2
25 Shadow of Napalm
26 Plunderbird 4
27 Sir Chromalot
28 Wel'dor
29 Dreadnaut XP-1
30 Stinger
31 Centurion
32 Suicidal Tendencies

Battle Board

Heat A

Medusa 2000

Attila the Drum King B3

Indefatigable

Chaos 2 atomic

Heat B

Velocirippa

Robochicken Razer

Milly-ann Bug

Pussycat Reptirron

Eliminator

Medusa 2000

Manchester

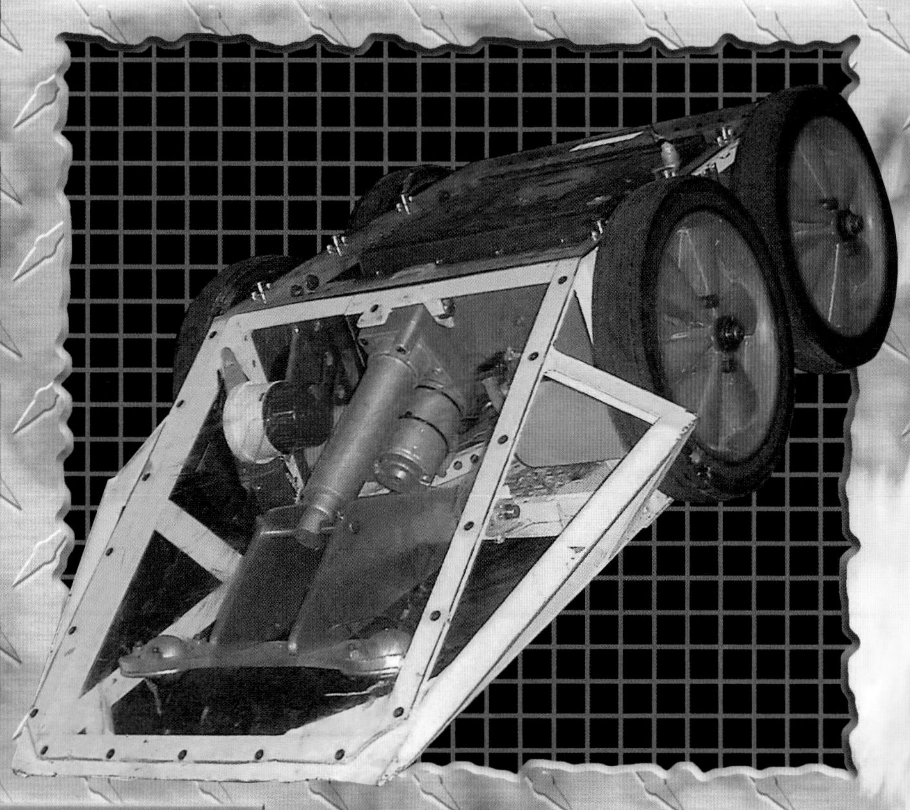

Weight	75.4kg
Dimensions	0.99m x 0.6m x 0.3m
Speed	10mph
Turning Circle	0m
Clearance	50mm
Power	4 motors made from scrap computer parts. 2 x 12v batteries
Weapons	Rear rotating weapon with blades. Front lifter
Notes	Coloured fluorescent green and orange
Previous Form	First-time competitors
Team	Don Weir (captain), Graham Baron and Michael Baron

Attila the Drum

Southampton

74.4kg	Weight
1.3m x 0.9m x 0.5m	Dimensions
12–15mph	Speed
0m	Turning Circle
25mm	Clearance
2 x 24v motors	Power
Mace and pickaxe	Weapons
Kevlar body. Fully floating electronics. Runs both ways up	Notes
First-time competitors	Previous Form
Berny Ryder (captain), Tony Knapp and Ayse Knapp	Team

King B3 (seed 17)

Essex

Weight	77.3kg
Dimensions	1m x 0.8m x 0.25m
Speed	14mph
Turning Circle	0m
Clearance	50mm
Power	2 x 750-watt, 24v motors
Weapons	Petrol-powered 20cm saw. Electric lifting/flipping spikes
Notes	Cost £4,000 to make
Previous Form	Series 2: beat All Torque in heat final. Knocked out by Road Block in 2nd round of semi-final. Series 3: beaten by 101 in heat final
Team	Simon Harrison (captain), Tony Sharp and Grant Hornsby

Indefatigable

Shropshire

78.5kg	Weight
1.5m x 0.75m x 0.5m	Dimensions
15mph	Speed
0m	Turning Circle
60–70mm	Clearance
2 x 12v batteries. 2 wheelchair motors	Power
2 lifting spikes	Weapons
Parts taken from quarry trucks, recycled phone boxes and wheely bins. Built in 5 weeks for £400	Notes
First-time competitors	Previous Form

Brian Olliver (captain), Richard Pitman and Daniel Lloyd **Team**

Chaos 2 (seed 1)
Ipswich

Weight	79.4kg
Dimensions	0.9m x 0.71m x 0.38m
Speed	12mph
Turning Circle	0m
Clearance	1mm
Power	2 lawnmower motors
Weapons	Gas flipper powered by a fire extinguisher
Notes	Built in 6 months for £250. Made from aluminium and polycarbonate
Previous Form	Series 1: finalist. Series 2: lost to Mace in heat final. Series 3: overall winner
Team	George Francis (captain), Ian Swann and Richard Swann

Atomic

Arley, Worcester

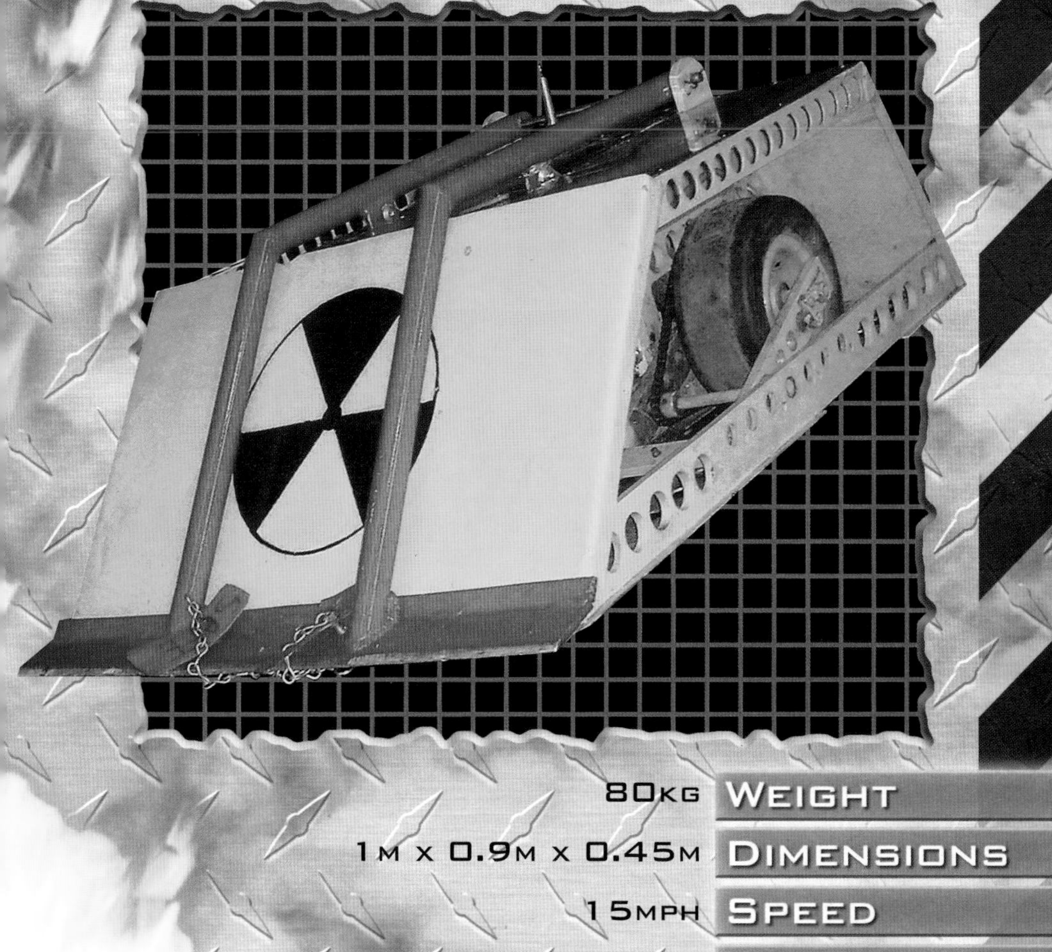

80kg	Weight
1m x 0.9m x 0.45m	Dimensions
15mph	Speed
0m	Turning Circle
20mm	Clearance
2 x 24v motors	Power
Flipper Blade	Weapons
Shell made of scrap aluminium. Total cost of robot £1,000	Notes
First-time competitors	Previous Form
Stephen Bebb (captain), David Bebb and Paul Francis	Team

Velocirippa

Nottingham

Weight	78.9kg
Dimensions	1m x 0.5m x 0.5m
Speed	20mph
Turning Circle	0m
Clearance	10mm
Power	Electric starter motor from a car
Weapons	Static front battering rams. Rear-spiked bumpers
Notes	Body is steel and armour-plated. Self-righting device
Previous Form	Series 3: beaten by Evil Weevil, Gnasher and The General in the final of the football competition
Team	Trevor Wright (captain), Matthew Wright and Anthony Hillier

Robochicken

Tiverton, Devon

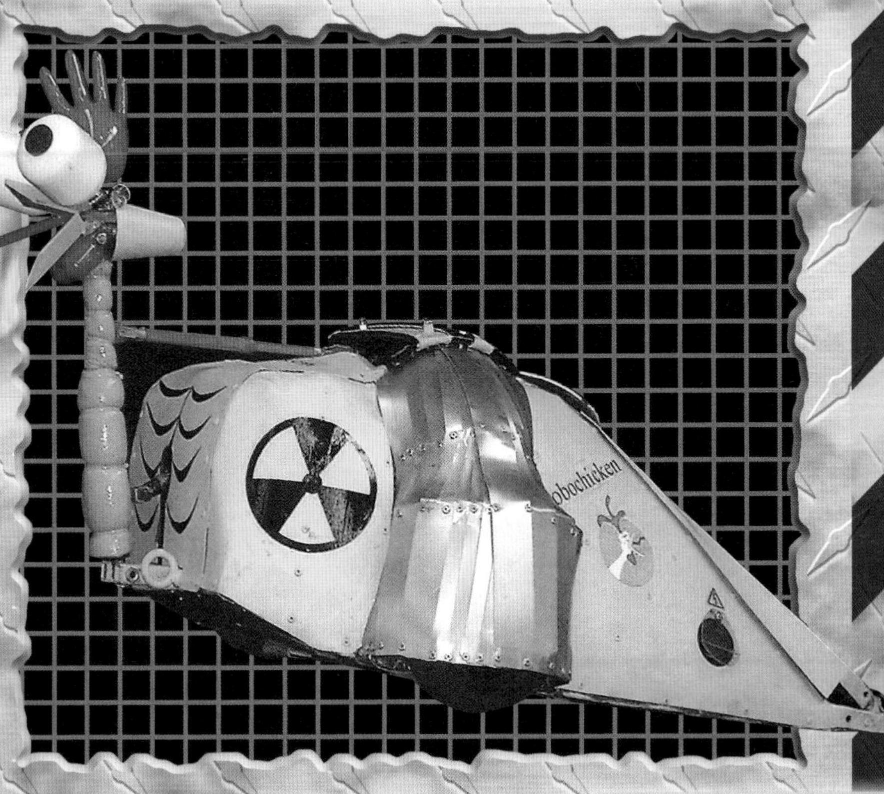

Weight	75kg
Dimensions	1.1m x 0.88m x 0.89m
Speed	8mph
Turning Circle	0m
Clearance	2mm at back, 10mm at front
Power	2 emergency light batteries
Weapons	Pneumatic flipper at rear and 'chicken's beak' at front
Notes	Shell and chassis of lightweight but tough sprung steel. The eyes are ballcocks and the crest is a rubber glove
Previous Form	First-time competitors
Team	Jason Snow (captain), Farren White and Alec Dick

Razer (seed 3)

Bournemouth

Weight	80kg
Dimensions	1.2m x 0.8m x 0.8m
Speed	11mph
Turning Circle	0m
Clearance	8mm
Power	2 x 12v batteries
Weapons	9-tonne hydraulic piercer
Notes	Highly sculptured aluminium and steel body. 450 holes drilled in the robot to keep its weight down
Previous Form	Reigning world and international champion. Series 2 & 3: best design award. Series 2: lost to Inquisition in heats. Series 3: pinball game champion
Team	Ian Lewis (captain), Simon Scott and Vincent Blood

Milly-Ann Bug

Leeds

Weight	79.3kg
Dimensions	1.2m x 0.75m x 0.6m
Speed	12mph
Turning Circle	1m
Clearance	65mm
Power	4 x 750-watt electric motors
Weapons	Spikes and Kevlar hair to gum up chainsaws
Notes	2 hemispherical pods with independent four-wheel drive. Steel chassis and the domes are made from bullet-proof jacket material
Previous Form	Series 2: most original entry. Series 3: fought Bumblebot in 1st round of heat – drove themselves down the pit
Team	Geoff Warren (captain), Gerry Warren and Liz Warren

Pussycat (seed 19)
Gloucester

Weight	79.7kg
Dimensions	0.76m x 0.43m x 0.56m
Speed	20mph
Turning Circle	0m
Clearance	40mm
Power	2 x 750-watt Bosch motors
Weapons	Circular blade powered by a Bosch motor
Notes	Shell is made of aluminium and polycarbonate, hand-painted by Alan
Previous Form	Series 1: beaten by Road Block in Grand Final. Series 3: beaten by Scutter's Revenge in heat final
Team	Robin Herrick (captain), Alan Gribble, Robert Bettington and David Gribble

Reptirron

Forest of Dean, Gloucestershire

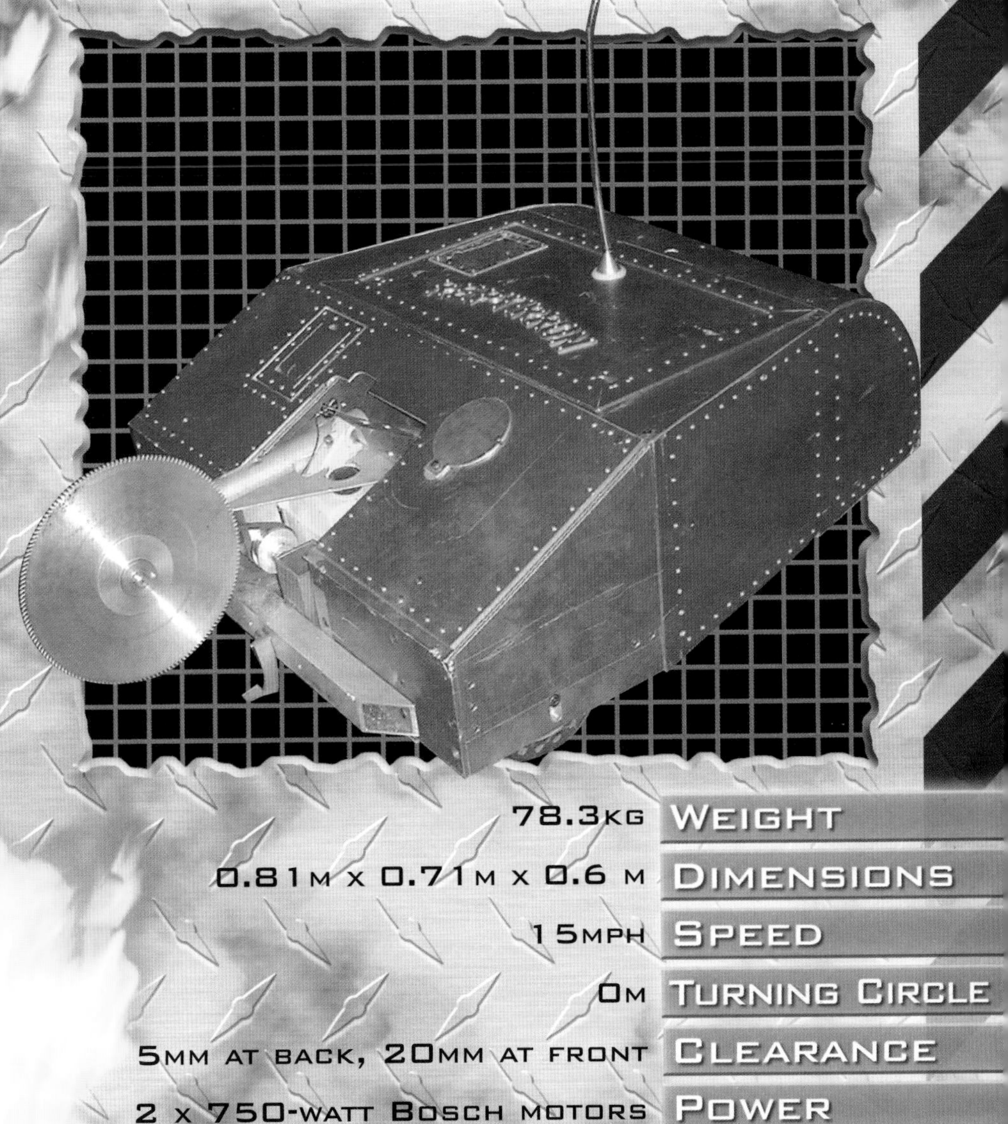

78.3kg	Weight
0.81m x 0.71m x 0.6 m	Dimensions
15mph	Speed
0m	Turning Circle
5mm at back, 20mm at front	Clearance
2 x 750-watt Bosch motors	Power
Circular saw	Weapons
Aluminium chassis	Notes
First-time competitors	Previous Form
Gordon Townley (captain) and Stuart Townley	Team

Battle Board

Heat C

Fire Storm II

The Morgue
Scar

Bolt from the Blue

Djótóir
Ming II

Heat D

Crusader 2

Steg 2
Cronos

Mazakari

Iron-Awe
Mortis

Eliminator

Fire Storm II

(seed 5) Durham

79.9kg	Weight
0.29m x 0.97m x 0.82m	Dimensions
15mph	Speed
0m	Turning Circle
6mm (adjustable)	Clearance
3 x 12v batteries	Power
Flipping arm powered by a CO_2 fire extinguisher	Weapons
Built in 3 months for £2,000. Very manoeuverable due to go-kart wheels.	Notes
Series 2 (as Groundhog): knocked out by Cassius in heat final. Series 3: won heat against Diotóir and semi-final against Panic Attack. Knocked out in 1st round of Grand Final by Chaos 2	Previous Form
Graham Bone (captain) and Alex Mordue	Team

The Morgue

Swansea

Weight	76.7kg
Dimensions	1.25m x 0.65m x 0.42m
Speed	12mph
Turning Circle	0m
Clearance	10mm
Power	2 x 24v, 750-watt Bosch motors
Weapons	Front shunt with lifting forks
Notes	Low centre of gravity due to egg shape. Kevlar shell. Forks use the same mechanism as adjustable beds
Previous Form	First-time competitors

Team	Dorian Caudy (captain), Mark Hooper and Huw White

Scar

Leamington Spa

79.5kg	Weight
0.9m x 0.8m x 0.34m	Dimensions
4–5mph	Speed
0m	Turning Circle
8mm	Clearance
2 wheelchair motors	Power
3 hardened-steel cutters at front	Weapons
Can be driven clockwise or anti-clockwise. Shell of steel/alloy plating	Notes
First-time competitors	Previous Form
Tony Adams (captain) and Chris Adams	Team

Bolt from the Blue

Lake District

Weight	79.4kg
Dimensions	1m x 0.7m x 0.4m
Speed	10mph
Turning Circle	0m
Clearance	0mm
Power	2 x 12v batteries. 2 wheelchair motors
Weapons	Flipper arm
Notes	Compressed air powers the arm
Previous Form	First-time competitors
Team	James Proctor (captain), Chris Elleray and Lucien Proctor

(Seed 21) Diótóir
Eire

80kg	Weight
0.8m x 0.8m x 0.4m	Dimensions
8mph	Speed
0m	Turning Circle
0–2mm (adjustable)	Clearance
3 x 12v batteries	Power
Hydraulic crushing and flipping arm	Weapons
Covered in fur. The roboteers wear matching waistcoats	Notes
Series 1: beaten by Road Block in heat final. Series 2 (as Nemesis): beaten by Onslaught in heat final. Series 3: beaten by Fire Storm in heat final	Previous Form
Peter Redmond (captain) and Cairon Byrne	Team

Ming II

West Cranmore, nr Bath

Weight	80.2kg
Dimensions	1.3m x 0.78m 0.28m
Speed	15mph
Turning Circle	0m
Clearance	13mm
Power	2 x 12v batteries
Weapons	Two spikes each side and a flipper
Notes	Aluminium chassis. Nose moves upwards
Previous Form	Series 3: knocked out by Mortis in 1st round of heat but would like to fight them again!
Team	Andrew Cotterell (captain), Alexander Cotterell and Oliver Cotterell

Crusader 2

Loughton, Essex

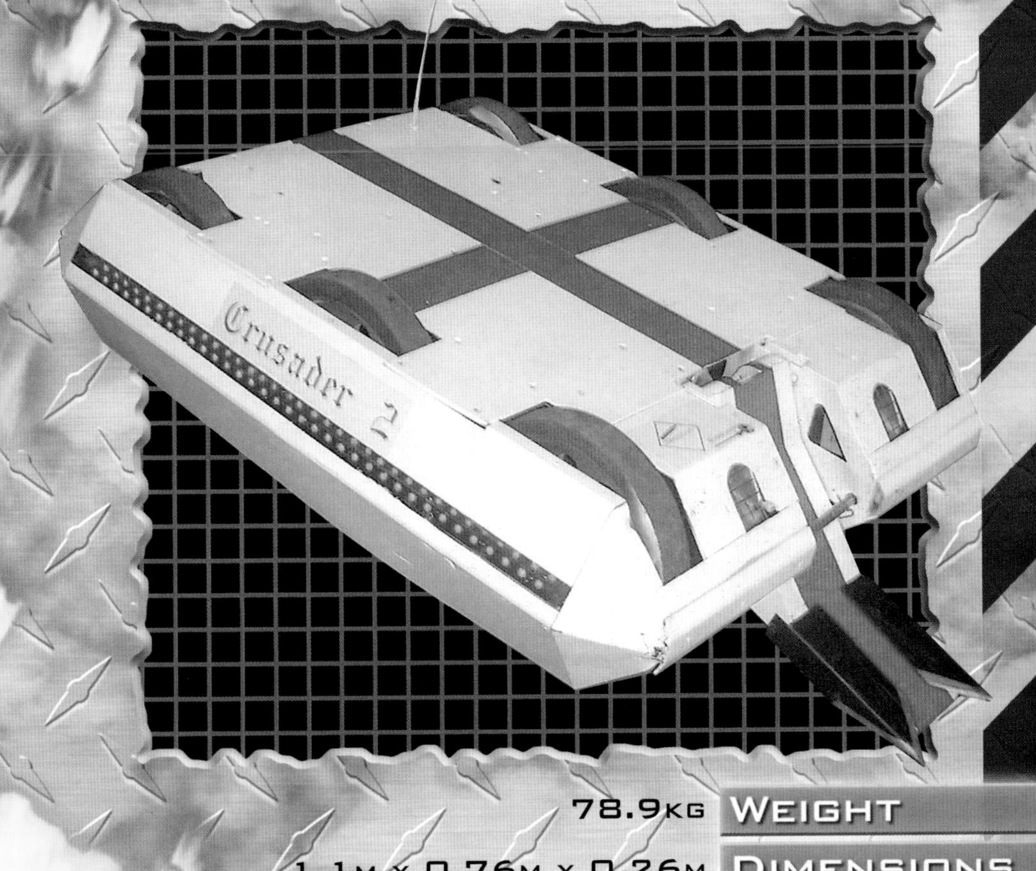

78.9kg	Weight
1.1m x 0.76m x 0.26m	Dimensions
8mph	Speed
0m	Turning Circle
5mm	Clearance
2 x 24v EMD motors	Power
Pneumatic lifting ram with 2 spikes. Can lift the robot's own weight	Weapons
Polycarbonate shell, steel chassis. 6 aluminium wheels. Processor controlled	Notes
Series 3: 3rd in Pinball competition	Previous Form
Richard Jessop (captain), Reg Claydon and Chris Williams	Team

STEG 2 (SEED 7)

HAMPSHIRE

WEIGHT	80KG
DIMENSIONS	0.86M X 0.70M X 0.35M
SPEED	15MPH
TURNING CIRCLE	0M
CLEARANCE	8MM
POWER	2 X 750-WATT BOSCH MOTORS
WEAPONS	PNEUMATIC CO_2-POWERED FLIPPER
NOTES	MADE OF AEROSPACE ALUMINIUM AND POLYCARBONATE
PREVIOUS FORM	SERIES 3 (AS STEG-O-SAW-US): PULLED FROM RESERVES TO COMPETE. WON HEAT AND SEMI-FINAL. KNOCKED OUT BY HYPNO-DISC IN GRAND FINAL
TEAM	ROB HEASMAN (CAPTAIN), DAN KING AND PETER ROWE

Cronos

Southampton

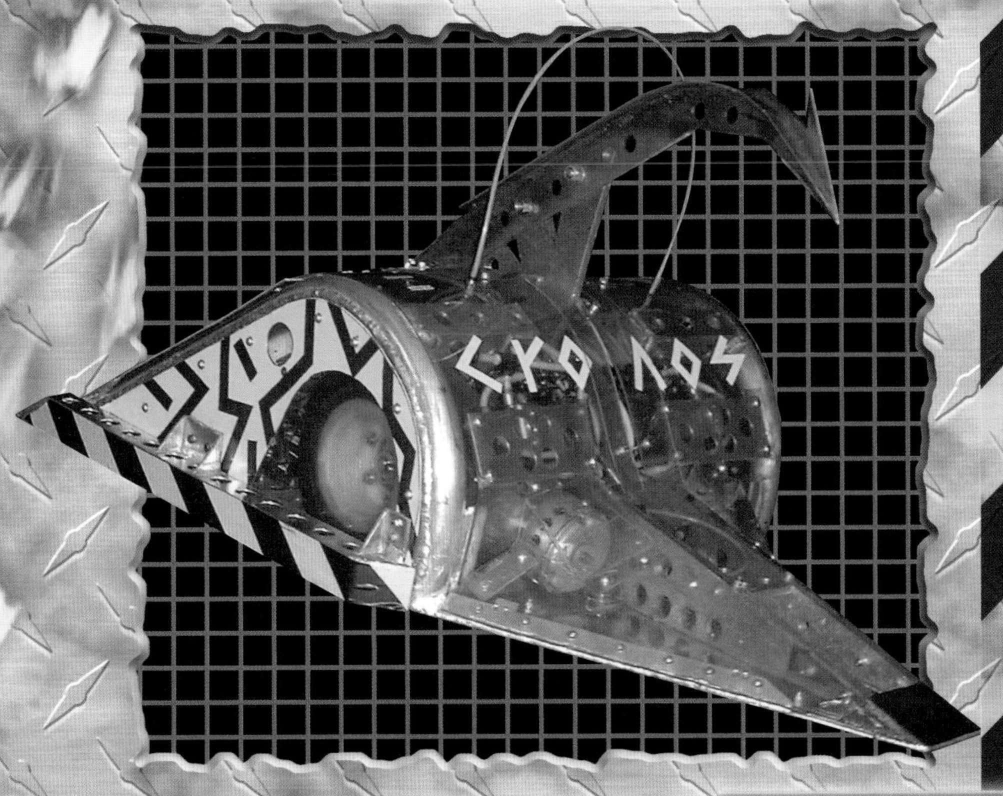

80.3kg	Weight
1.38m x 0.63m x 0.63m	Dimensions
12mph	Speed
0m	Turning Circle
4mm	Clearance
2 x 750-watt Bosch motors	Power
Pneumatic crusher, 7,500kg force. Pneumatic lifter, could lift a bus!	Weapons
Pneumatics powered by 12 air bags. Shell is composite aircraft-grade aluminium and macralon. 2 go-kart wheels	Notes
Series 3 (as Zeus): knocked out by Scutter's Revenge in 1st round of heats	Previous Form
Julian Raffle (captain) and Mark Raffle	Team

Mazakari

Hurworth, Darlington

Weight	79.9kg
Dimensions	1.4m x 0.74m x 0.3m
Speed	6mph
Turning Circle	0m
Clearance	15mm
Power	2 wheelchair scooter motors
Weapons	Custom-built solid steel 70cm diameter disc with attached blades
Notes	Custom-built steel wheels. Solid steel chassis, 3mm aluminium check plate
Previous Form	First-time competitors

Team Phill Sievers (captain), Phil Neely and Richard Neely

IRON-AWE

SOMERSET

79.3KG	WEIGHT
1M X 0.7M X 0.7M	DIMENSIONS
6MPH	SPEED
0M	TURNING CIRCLE
8MM	CLEARANCE
2 X 750-WATT BOSCH MOTORS. 2 X HAWKER SBS 15 BATTERIES	POWER
GREAT BIG AXE	WEAPONS
MOST PARTS ARE FROM PACKAGING MACHINERY	NOTES
FIRST-TIME COMPETITORS	PREVIOUS FORM
GILBERT GRIMM (CAPTAIN) AND ROBERT GRIMM	TEAM

MORTIS (SEED 23)

NOTTINGHAMSHIRE AND CAMBRIDGESHIRE

WEIGHT	79.3KG
DIMENSIONS	0.76M X 0.91M X 0.36M
SPEED	12MPH
TURNING CIRCLE	0M
CLEARANCE	50MM
POWER	3 X DC BRUSHLESS 3-PHASE SERVOS
WEAPONS	AXE AND LIFTER
NOTES	CAN LIFT 100KG. USES AEROSPACE-GRADE MATERIALS
PREVIOUS FORM	SERIES 1: LOST HEAT FINAL TO RECYCLOPSE ON A JUDGE'S DECISION. SERIES 2: BEAT OBLIVION TO WIN HEAT FINAL. KNOCKED OUT BY PANIC ATTACK IN SEMI-FINAL. SERIES 3: BEATEN BY GRAVEDIGGER IN 2ND ROUND OF HEATS
TEAM	ROB KNIGHT (CAPTAIN), ARTHUR CHILCOTT AND PAUL FORD

Battle Board

Heat E

Dominator 2

Henry 2 | 101

Shadow of Napalm

Disc-O-Inferno | Major Tom

Heat F

Tornado

Kater Killer | Gemini

Inverterbrat

The Creature | Berserk 2

Eliminator

Dominator 2

Cambridgeshire

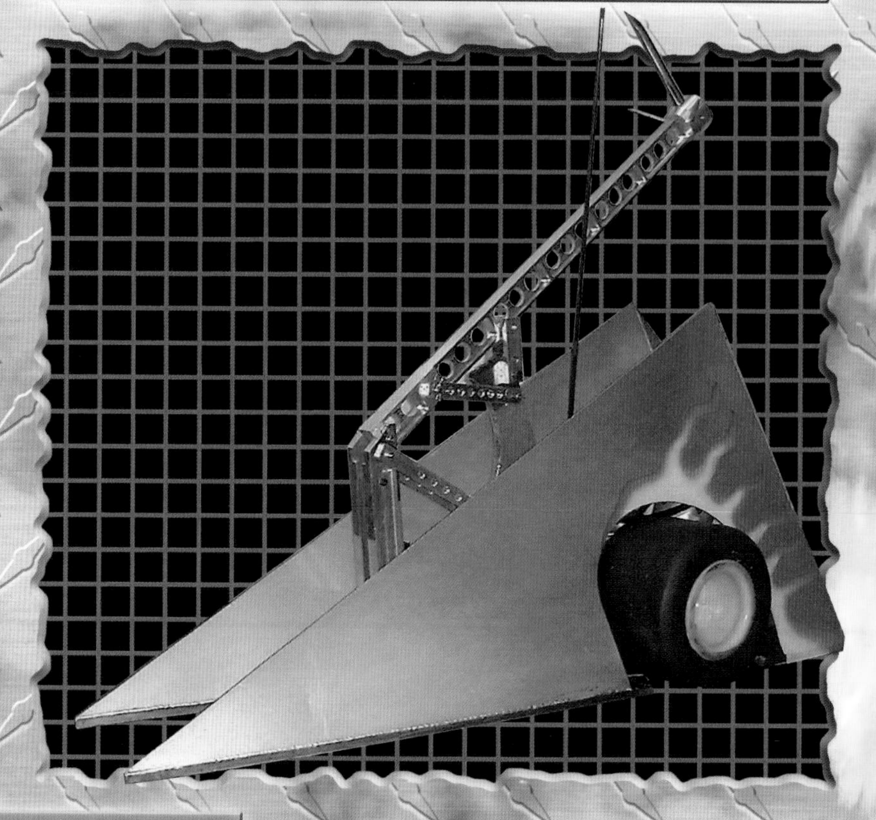

Weight	79.9kg
Dimensions	1.4m x 0.8m x 0.65m
Speed	20mph
Turning Circle	0m
Clearance	10mm
Power	2 industrial motors
Weapons	Pneumatic axe
Notes	Plasma-nitride-coated titanium
Previous Form	Series 3: came second to Razer in Pinball competition

Team Peter Halloway (captain), Chris Hall and Paul Tolliday

HENRY 2

WOODBRIDGE, SUFFOLK

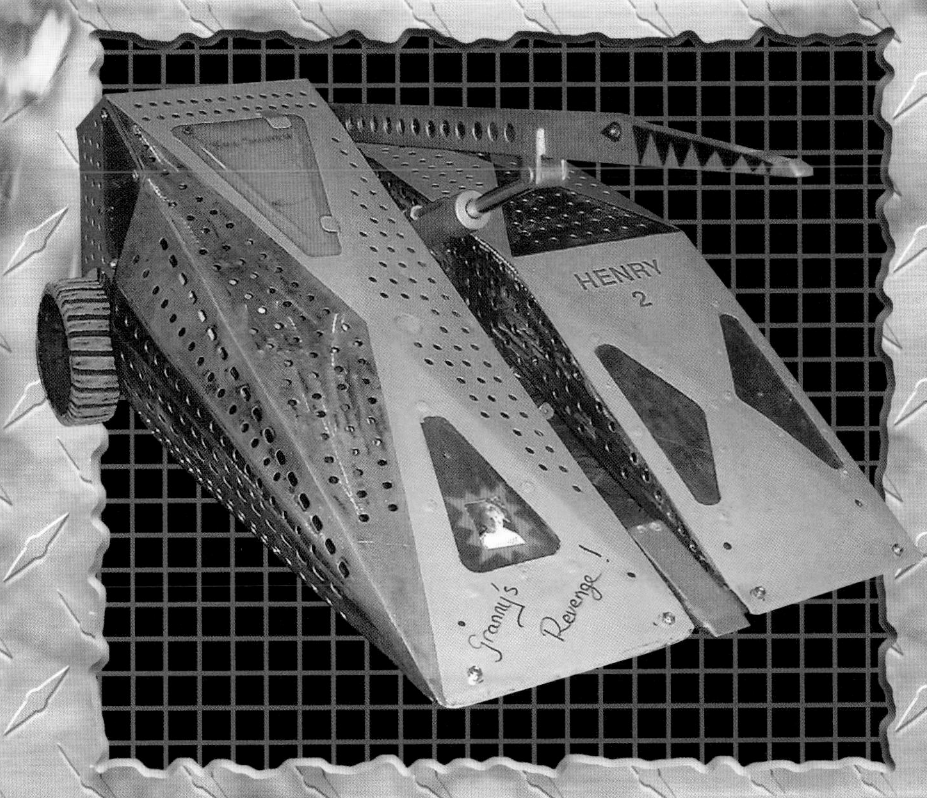

80.1KG	WEIGHT
1.1M X 0.85M X 0.5M	DIMENSIONS
15MPH	SPEED
0M	TURNING CIRCLE
3MM	CLEARANCE
PETROL ENGINE DRIVES A HYDRAULIC PUMP THAT DRIVES SPOOL VALVES	POWER
HYDRAULIC RAM	WEAPONS
STEEL SHELL, 2 GO-KART WHEELS. SOME PARTS FROM A RELIANT ROBIN. PHOTO OF GRANDMA ON FRONT!	NOTES
SERIES 3 (AS HENRY): KNOCKED OUT BY STEG-O-SAW-US IN 2ND ROUND OF HEAT	PREVIOUS FORM
TOM MOYE (CAPTAIN), LEON MOYE AND MELANIE MOYE	TEAM

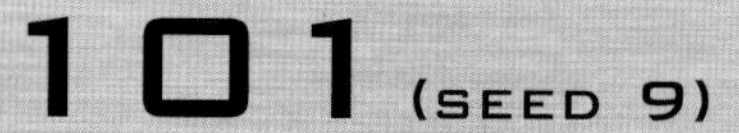

101 (Seed 9)

Kettering

Weight	77.7kg
Dimensions	1m x 0.75m x 0.25m
Speed	8mph
Turning Circle	0m
Clearance	50mm
Power	2 industrial motors
Weapons	200mph spike powered by CO_2; can sense distances to objects
Notes	Aircraft-grade aluminium shell. Tracks from a milk bottle washing machine. Uses racing-car batteries
Previous Form	Series 2 (as Robo-Doc): lost to King Buxton in heat final. Series 3: won heat. lost to Hypno-Disc in semi-final
Team	Mike Franklin (captain) and Amy Franklin

Shadow of Napalm

(Seed 25) Dartford

75.3kg	Weight
0.91m x 0.76m x 0.46m	Dimensions
10mph	Speed
0m	Turning Circle
0–50mm	Clearance
2 x 12v 35a motors	Power
Large spike and lifting mechanism	Weapons
Kevlar shell with aluminium decking and titanium. Low-profile wheelchair wheels	Notes
Series 2: won heat, eliminated in trials for semi-final. Series 3: knocked out by Steg-O-Saw-Us in heat final	Previous Form
David Crosby (captain), Clare Greenway and Victoria Allgood	Team

Disc-O-Inferno

York University

Weight	80.2kg
Dimensions	1.2m x 0.7m x 0.3m
Speed	8mph
Turning Circle	0m
Clearance	25mm
Power	3 x 750-watt bosch motors
Weapons	700rpm flywheel with 2 x 15cm blades
Notes	Can run upside down. Shell is 6mm polycarbonate, chassis is welded aluminium
Previous Form	First-time competitors

Team Mark Marshall (captain), Nick Bullock and Oliver Reed-Smith

Major Tom

Isle of Sheppey

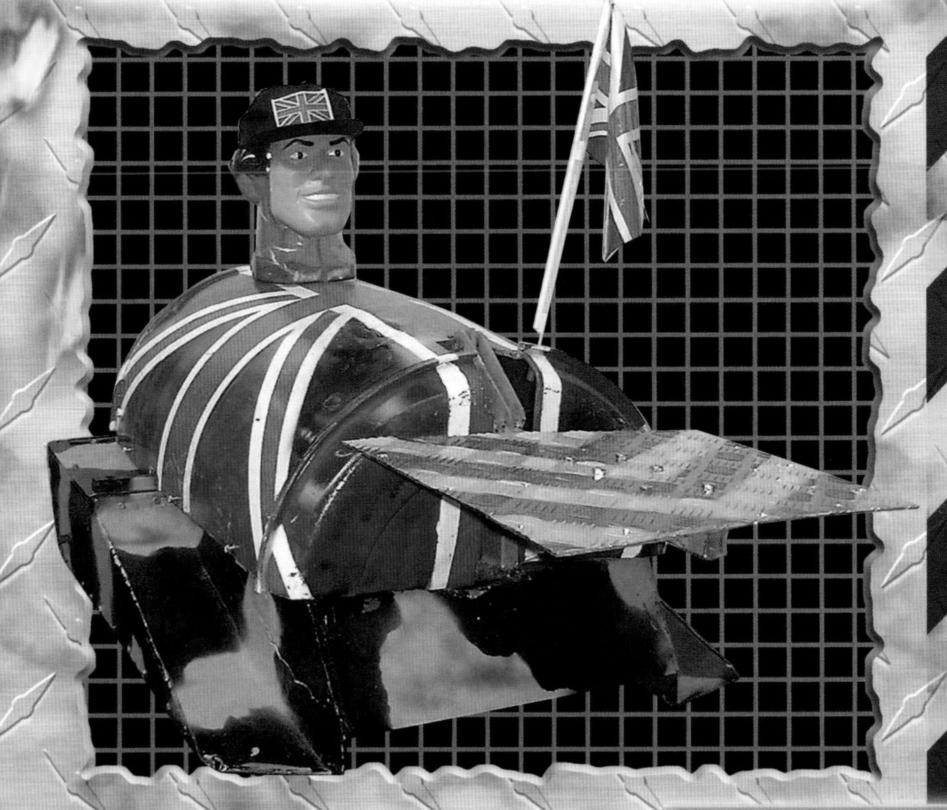

80.1kg	Weight
0.91m x 0.76m x 0.61m	Dimensions
10mph	Speed
0m	Turning Circle
5mm	Clearance
2 golf-caddy motors	Power
Powered ramp	Weapons
Made from bicycles, golf caddies and lawnmowers. Main body is a garden water barrel. Head is Captain Cosmic, from a bubblegum machine	Notes
First-time competitors	Previous Form
Henry Ryan (captain), Arthur Robinson and Gerald Morris	Team

Tornado

Huntingdon, Cambridgeshire

Weight	78.2kg
Dimensions	0.85m x 0.7m x 0.25m
Speed	10mph
Turning Circle	0m
Clearance	25mm
Power	2 x Industrial motors: 7bhp
Weapons	Pneumatic spike, fixed spikes
Notes	The ram came from a loudspeaker production line. Made from welded steel and polycarbonate
Previous Form	First-time competitors

Team Andrew Marchant (captain), David Gamble and Bryan Moss

Kater Killer

Addlestone, Surrey

80kg	Weight
0.6m x 0.75m x 1.1m	Dimensions
10mph	Speed
0m	Turning Circle
30mm	Clearance
2 x 12a batteries, 2 x 800-watt motors, 2 x 7,500 newton linear actuators	Power
A flipper lifting arm with spikes	Weapons
Tracked: rubber with aluminium pads. Bulletproof shell of macralon and lexan	Notes
Series 3: knocked out in first round of heat by Napalm	Previous Form
Keith Williams (captain), Georje Reed and Julie-Ann Williams	Team

Gemini (seed 8)

Hastings

Weight	80kg
Dimensions	Each 0.74m x 0.7m x 0.38m
Speed	5–6mph
Turning Circle	0m
Clearance	15mm
Power	4 wheelchair motors
Weapons	Pneumatic flippers, each can flip 250kg
Notes	Cluster bot: identical twins competing together. Shells are fibreglass and Kevlar
Previous Form	Series 2 (as Mace): eliminated in the gauntlet of semi-final. Series 3 (as Mace II): beaten by Chaos 2 in semi-final
Team	Shane Howard (captain), Brian Fountain and Darryl Howard

Invertebrat

Surrey

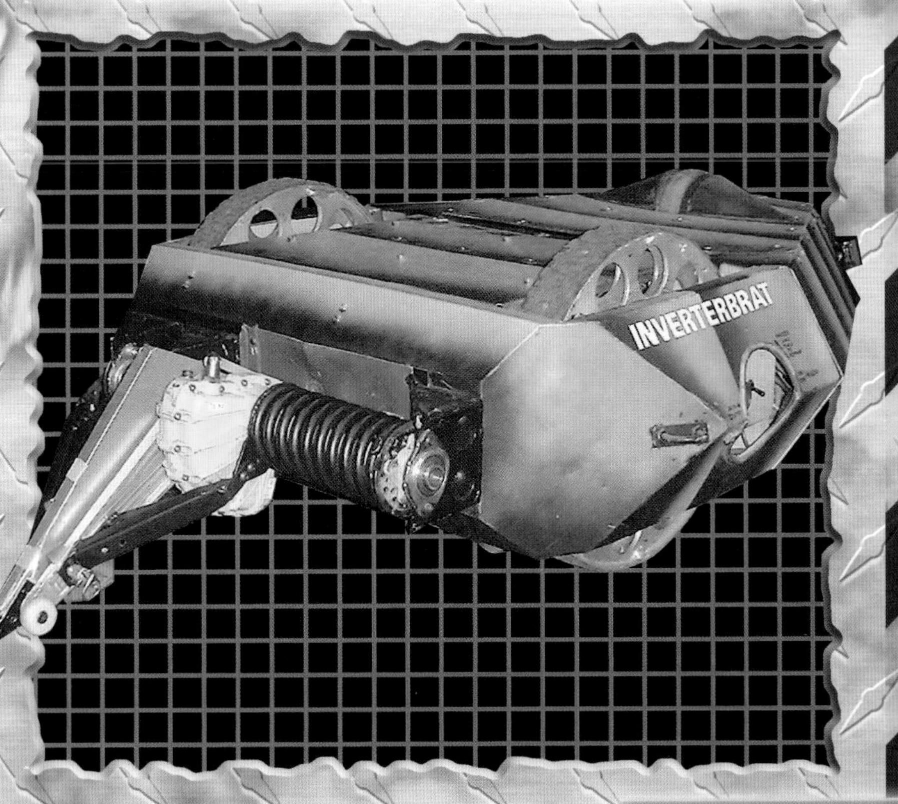

79.3kg	Weight
1.4m x 0.8m x 0.35m	Dimensions
10mph	Speed
0m	Turning Circle
50mm	Clearance
2 x wheelchair motors	Power
Pneumatic flipper. Rotating bludgeoner	Weapons
Parts are from scrap yards and manufacturers	Notes
Series 3: lost heat final against Beast of bodmin due to an electrical fault	Previous Form
Peter Bignell (captain) and les Wall	Team

The Creature

Rhyl, North Wales

Weight	78.3kg
Dimensions	1.2m x 0.8m x 0.6m
Speed	10mph
Turning Circle	0m
Clearance	40mm
Power	2 x wheelchair motors
Weapons	Mechanically operated forklift
Notes	Local wheelchair manufacturer donated the motors. Ten people invovled in construction
Previous Form	Series 3 (as Twn Twrn): knocked out in 1st round of heat by Trident

Team Mark Harmsworth (captain), Elanor Harmsworth and David Harmsworth

(SEED 24) BERSERK 2

HUDDERSFIELD

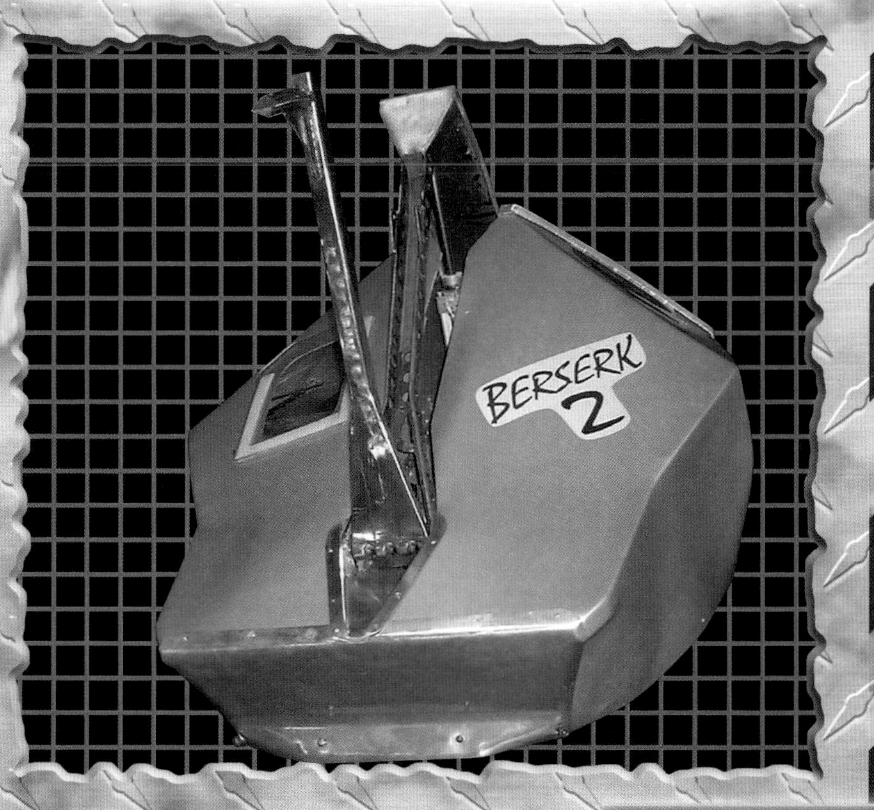

78.3KG	WEIGHT
0.92M x 0.91M x 0.69M	DIMENSIONS
6MPH	SPEED
0M	TURNING CIRCLE
45MM	CLEARANCE
PNEUMATIC – 1000PSI AIR PRESSURE	POWER
HAMMER AT FRONT, FORKLIFT AT REAR	WEAPONS
WEAPONS MADE FROM STEEL. BODY MADE OF FIBREGLASS	NOTES
SERIES 2: COMPETED IN HEAVYWEIGHT SHOWDOWN AGAINST SIREN, KICK ROBOT AND DEMON. SERIES 3: LOST TO HYPNO-DISC IN HEAT FINAL	PREVIOUS FORM
STUART FORD (CAPTAIN), GRAHAM KERSHAW AND CHRISTOPHER O'CONNELL	TEAM

Battle Board
Heat G

Kronic the Wedgehog

Gravedigger Thermidor II

Darke Destroyer II

War Hog dreadnaut XP-1

Heat H

Wheely Big Cheese

Prizephita mkII Wheelo-saurus

Suicidal Tendencies

Killertron Maverick

Eliminator

Kronic the Wedgehog

Devon

78.2kg	Weight
1m x 0.8m x 0.5m	Dimensions
10mph	Speed
0.8m	Turning Circle
1–12mm	Clearance
2 Sinclair-C5 motors	Power
Pneumatic flipper and spike	Weapons
Polycarbonate shell, steel and aluminium frame. 4 industrial trolley wheels. Contains bubble wrap!	Notes
First-time competitors	Previous Form

Dave Lang (captain), John Lang and Mike Gardner — Team

GRAVEDIGGER (SEED 13)

NORWICH

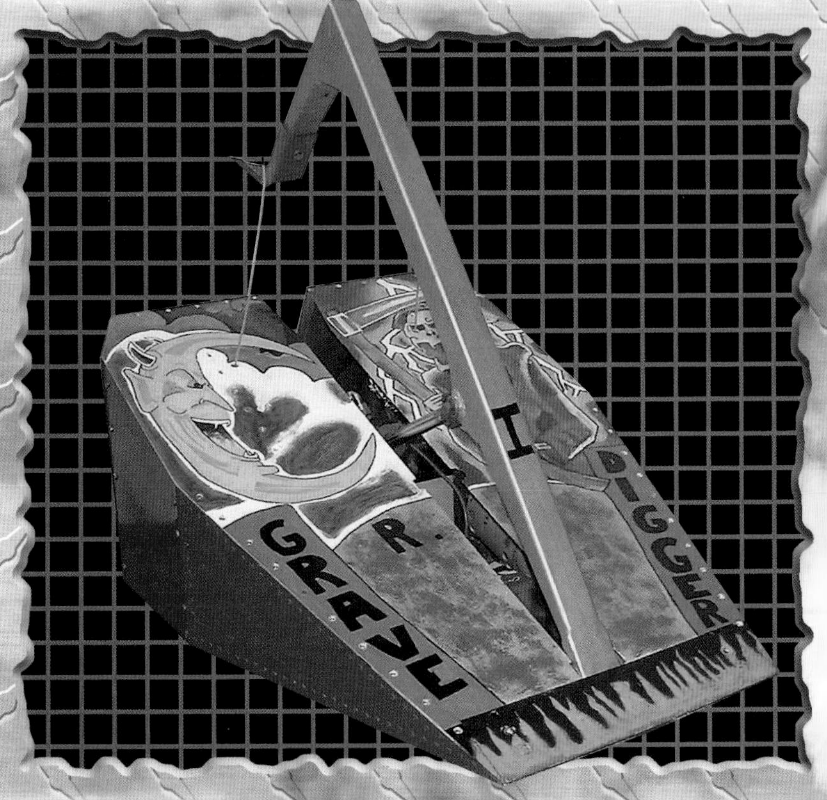

WEIGHT	75.7KG
DIMENSIONS	1.02M X 0.71M X 0.46M
SPEED	8MPH
TURNING CIRCLE	0M
CLEARANCE	8MM
POWER	2 X 750-WATT, 1HP MOTORS
WEAPONS	HYDRAULIC RAM OPERATING ARM
NOTES	BODY SHELL IS ALUMINIUM PLATING
PREVIOUS FORM	SERIES 3: WON HEAT FINAL. LOST TO STEG-O-SAW-US IN 1ST ROUND OF SEMI-FINAL
TEAM	JON CHAPLIN (CAPTAIN), OWEN RAMSEY AND DAVE CHAPLIN

Thermidor II

Norwich

79.9kg	**Weight**
1.3m x 0.7m x 0.325m	**Dimensions**
15mph	**Speed**
0m	**Turning Circle**
5–25mm	**Clearance**
2 x 750-watt Bosch motors	**Power**
Lobster claws and flipper	**Weapons**
Aluminium shell. 2 wheels from a Mini Metro	**Notes**
Series 3: pushed down the pit in 2nd round of heat by Scutter's Revenge	**Previous Form**
David Harding (captain), Ian Harvey and Eli Kirkpatrick	**Team**

Darke Destroyer II

Romsey, Hampshire

Weight	77.3kg
Dimensions	1.3m x 0.8m x 0.65m
Speed	15mph
Turning Circle	0m
Clearance	40mm
Power	Car starter motor
Weapons	Bulldozer front with spikes, high-speed spring-loaded axes, wedge back
Notes	Made from mild steel, aluminium and wood. Parts came from cars, go-karts and golf caddies
Previous Form	Series 3: lost to Gravedigger in heat final

Team Rob Darke (captain), Chris Darke and George Murrell

War Hog

Hull

79.6kg	Weight
0.8m x 0.8m x 0.43m	Dimensions
12mph	Speed
0m	Turning Circle
20mm	Clearance
12v battery, 2 x Corsa starter motors. Ford Granada starter motor for weapon	Power
Wheel spinning at 500rpm	Weapons
Shell of mild steel plate and aluminium	Notes
First-time competitors	Previous Form
Colin Hare (captain), Paul Stephenson and Mark Charmers	Team

DREADNAUT XP-1

NUNEATON (SEED 29)

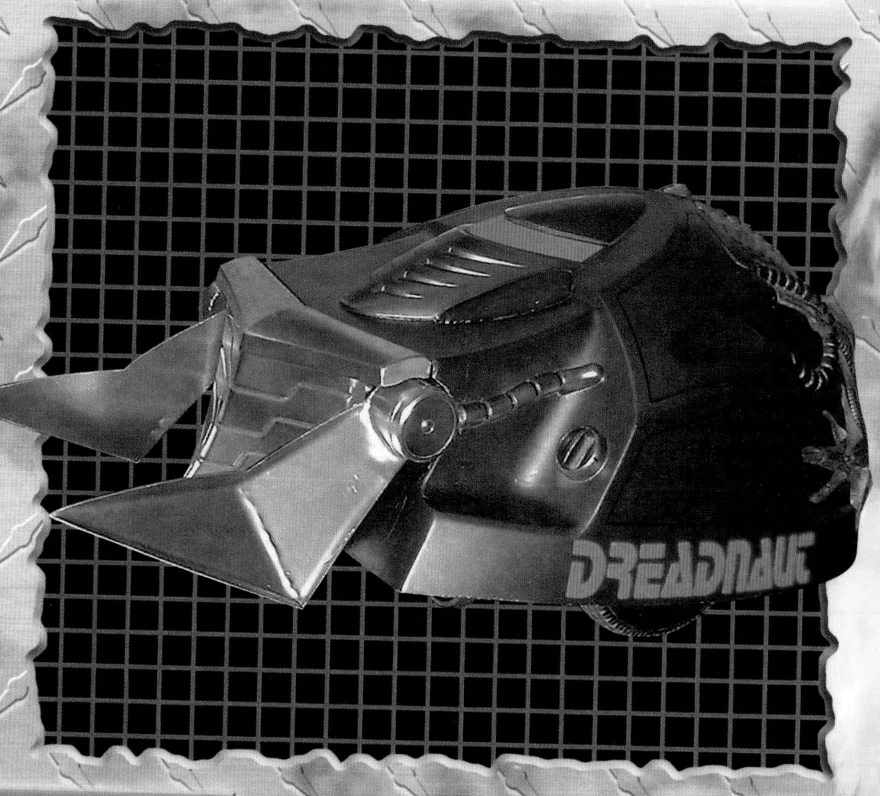

WEIGHT	77.6KG
DIMENSIONS	1.15M X 0.9M X 0.45M
SPEED	10MPH
TURNING CIRCLE	0M
CLEARANCE	100MM
POWER	2 WHEELCHAIR MOTORS
WEAPONS	LIFTING FORKS
NOTES	FIBREGLASS SHELL. 2 WHEELCHAIR WHEELS AND 2 CASTORS
PREVIOUS FORM	SERIES 1: LOST TO WEDGEHOG IN HEAT FINAL. SERIES 3: BEATEN BY TRIDENT IN HEAT FINAL
TEAM	KEN FELTWELL (CAPTAIN), DAVE VOWLES AND FAYE VOWLES

Wheely Big Cheese

(seed 15) Somerset

79.8kg	Weight
1.43m x 0.74m x 0.42m	Dimensions
6mph	Speed
0m	Turning Circle
6mm	Clearance
2 x 12v batteries	Power
Flipper powered by CO_2	Weapons
Made of bulletproof titanium. Flipper can lift up to 1 tonne	Notes
Series 3 (as Big Cheese): knocked out by Chaos 2 in 3rd round of heat	Previous Form
Roger Plant (captain) and Paul Otten	Team

Prizephita Mk II

Ipswich

Weight	78.9kg
Dimensions	1m x 0.95m x 0.5m
Speed	15mph
Turning Circle	0m
Clearance	5mm
Power	2 x 750-watt Bosch lawnmower motors
Weapons	Pneumatic flipper and spike, CO_2 powered
Notes	Polycarbonate shell. Bodywork is aluminium and steel. Wheelchair speed controllers
Previous Form	Series 3: knocked out by Thing in 1st round of heat

Team Roy Alcock (captain), Sharon Alcock and Phillip Chaplin

Wheelosaurus

Guildford, Surrey

76.5kg	Weight
1.5m x 1.5m x 0.75m	Dimensions
8mph	Speed
0m	Turning Circle
50mm	Clearance
2 wheelchair motors	Power
Petrol engine strimmer with brushwood cutter	Weapons
Victorian pram wheels with spikes. Peter refers to it as a 'grunge bot'	Notes
Series 2: attacked Sgt Bash, punctured his gas cylinder. Knocked out by Chaos in heat final	Previous Form
Peter Gibson (captain)	Team

KILLERTRON

MAIDSTONE, KENT

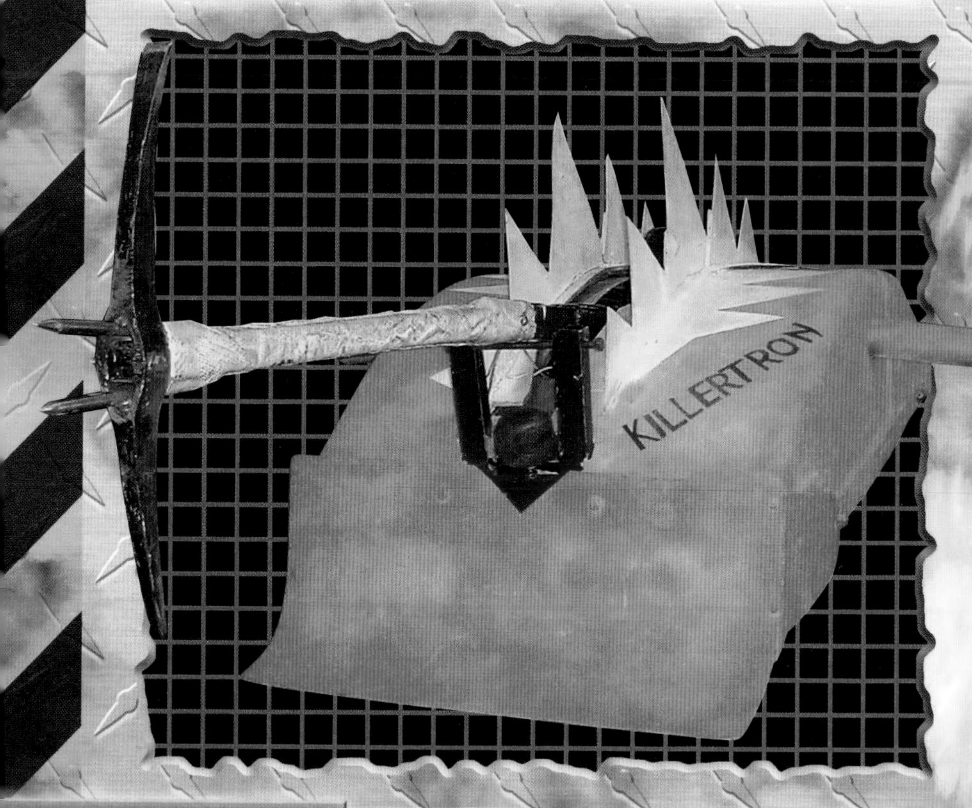

WEIGHT	80KG
DIMENSIONS	1.12M X 1.17M X 0.71M
SPEED	15MPH
TURNING CIRCLE	0M
CLEARANCE	77MM
POWER	2 X 24V WHEELCHAIR MOTORS
WEAPONS	BIG AXE
NOTES	MADE FROM THE LID OF A WHEELY BIN
PREVIOUS FORM	SERIES 1: KNOCKED OUT BY ROAD BLOCK IN HEAT FINAL. SERIES 2: WON HEAT AND SEMI-FINAL. KNOCKED OUT BY PANIC ATTACK IN FINAL PLAYOFF. SERIES 3: THIRD PLACE IN GRAND FINAL.
TEAM	RICHARD BROAD (CAPTAIN), ABDUL DEGIA AND IAN DEGIA

SUICIDAL TENDENCIES

(SEED 32) DERBY

80.2KG	WEIGHT
1.3M x 0.58M x 0.3M	DIMENSIONS
10MPH	SPEED
0M	TURNING CIRCLE
15MM	CLEARANCE
2 x 1,400-WATT MOTORS	POWER
PNEUMATIC AXE AND FRONT FORKLIFT	WEAPONS
BULLETPROOF METAL SHELL. TRACKED : HANDBUILT FROM ALUMINIUM. STEAM-ENGINE WHISTLE WHEN THE AXE STRIKES	NOTES
SERIES 3: LOST TO MACE 2 IN HEAT FINAL	PREVIOUS FORM
ANDREW JEFFREY (CAPTAIN), MARTIN JEFFREY AND CHARLES BINNS	TEAM

Maverick

Southampton

Weight	79.8kg
Dimensions	0.88m x 0.74m x 0.4m
Speed	6mph
Turning Circle	0m
Clearance	6mm
Power	2 wheelchair motors
Weapons	Pneumatic front flipper
Notes	Aluminium shell and plastic armour
Previous Form	First-time competitors

Team Francis Gallagher (captain), Kevin Gallagher and Brett Skinner

Battle Board
Heat I

Destruct-a-Bubble

Killerhurtz   Eric

Centurion

Splinter   Small Torque

Heat J

Bigger Brother

Clawed Hopper   Hammer & Tong

Spikasaurus

Bulldog Breed 2   Stinger

Eliminator

Destruct-a-Bubble

Chelmsford, Essex

Weight	77.3kg
Dimensions	1m truncated sphere
Speed	5mph
Turning Circle	0m
Clearance	26mm
Power	2 electric-wheelchair motors
Weapons	Pneumatic lance
Notes	Carbon fibre and Kevlar shell. 2 wheels off a small tractor. Other parts include a fire extinguisher
Previous Form	First-time competitors
Team	Bill Cozens (captain), Lawrence Cozens and Malcolm Burrells

(SEED 16) KILLERHURTZ

OXFORD

80KG	WEIGHT
1.2M x 0.8M x 0.3M	DIMENSIONS
16MPH	SPEED
0M	TURNING CIRCLE
40MM	CLEARANCE
2 x 750-WATT BOSCH MOTORS	POWER
PNEUMATIC AXE AND A HARDENED STEEL BLADE ON THE FRONT	WEAPONS
POLYCARBONATE SHELL, GO-PED WHEELS, CAR-STYLE STEERING	NOTES
SERIES 2: KNOCKED OUT BY ROAD BLOCK IN HEAT FINAL. SERIES 3: DROVE THEMSELVES STRAIGHT INTO THE PIT IN 1ST ROUND OF HEATS	PREVIOUS FORM
JOHN REID (CAPTAIN), DOMINIC PARKINSON AND REBECCA REASTON-BROWN	TEAM

Eric

Franfield, East Sussex

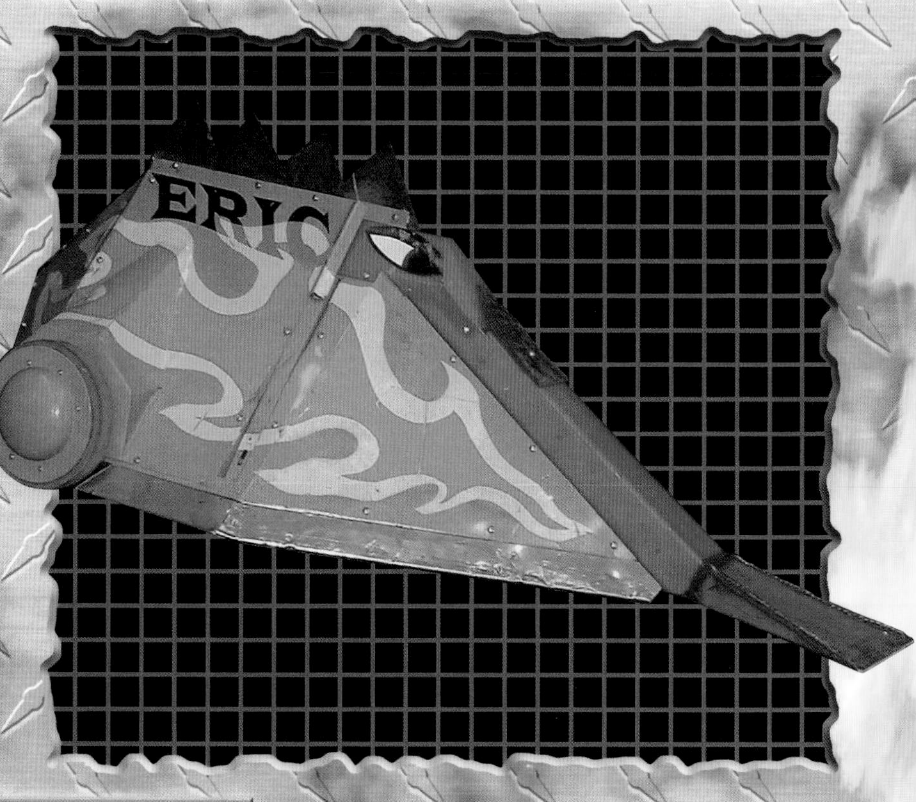

Weight	80.1kg
Dimensions	1.35m x 0.75m x 0.55m
Speed	10mph
Turning Circle	2m
Clearance	10mm
Power	2 wheelchair motors
Weapons	Hydraulic lifting jaw and can crush
Notes	Stainless steel shell. Starter motor from a grass cutting machine
Previous Form	Series 3: drove straight into the pit due to driver error in 1st round of heats
Team	Mike Hammerton (captain), Ian Nicholson and Bruce Nicholson

(SEED 31) CENTURION

ESSEX

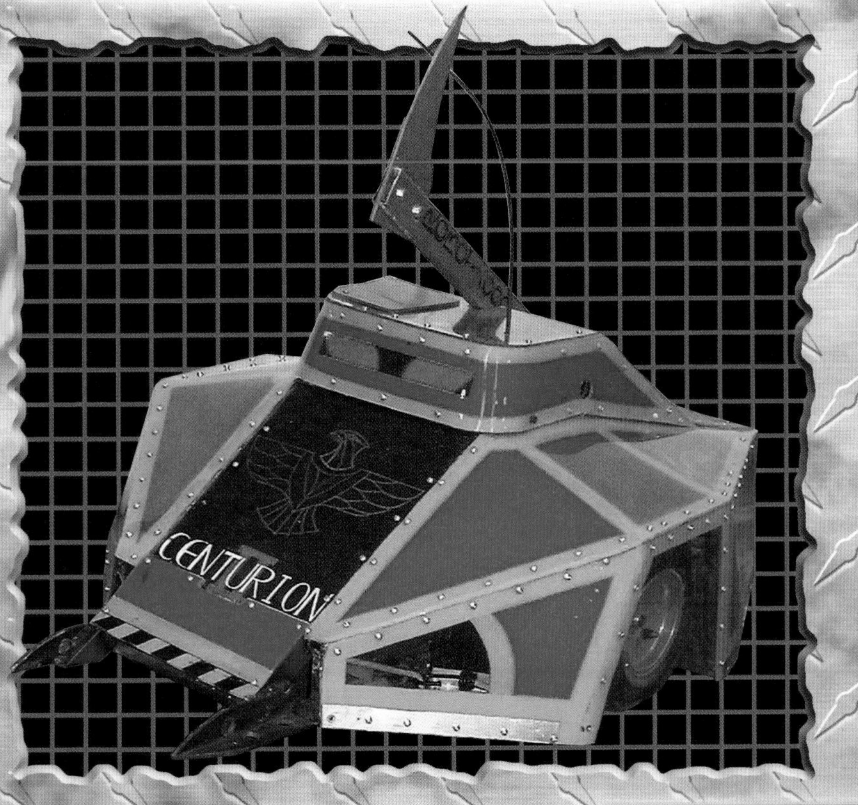

78.2KG	WEIGHT
1.1M X 0.8M X 0.5M	DIMENSIONS
15MPH	SPEED
0M	TURNING CIRCLE
10MM	CLEARANCE
2 INDUSTRIAL MOTORS	POWER
PNEUMATIC AXE. FRONT LIFTER – CAN LIFT 120KG	WEAPONS
MILD STEEL CHASSIS, POLYCARBONATE SHELL. 2 WET GO-KART WHEELS	NOTES
SERIES 3: KNOCKED OUT BY 101 IN 2ND ROUND OF HEATS	PREVIOUS FORM
RAY TAIT (CAPTAIN), MATHEW TAIT AND JEFF BRADFORD	TEAM

Splinter

Norwich

Weight	80.6kg
Dimensions	1m x 0.75m x 0.6m
Speed	15mph
Turning Circle	0m
Clearance	30mm
Power	2 x 750-watt, 24v motors
Weapons	Claws – wheelchair motor powered
Notes	Made from welded steel. One part is from a plastic oil drum
Previous Form	Series 2 (as Ivanhoe): knocked out by G.B.H. in heat final
Team	Stuart Weightman (captain) and Craig Weightman

Small Torque

Aberdour, nr Edinburgh

78.3kg	Weight
0.7m x 0.7m x 0.3m	Dimensions
20mph	Speed
0m	Turning Circle
50mm	Clearance
2 x 750-watt Bosch motors	Power
4,000rpm spinning disc and sharp teeth	Weapons
Bulletproof plastic shell. Wheels from a wheelbarrow. Special cooling system	Notes
Series 2 (as All Torque): knocked out by King Buxton in heat final. Series 3: knocked out by Thing in 2nd round of heats	Previous Form
Richie McBride (captain), Alex McBride and MArtyn Sloss	Team

Bigger Brother

Brighton (seed 14)

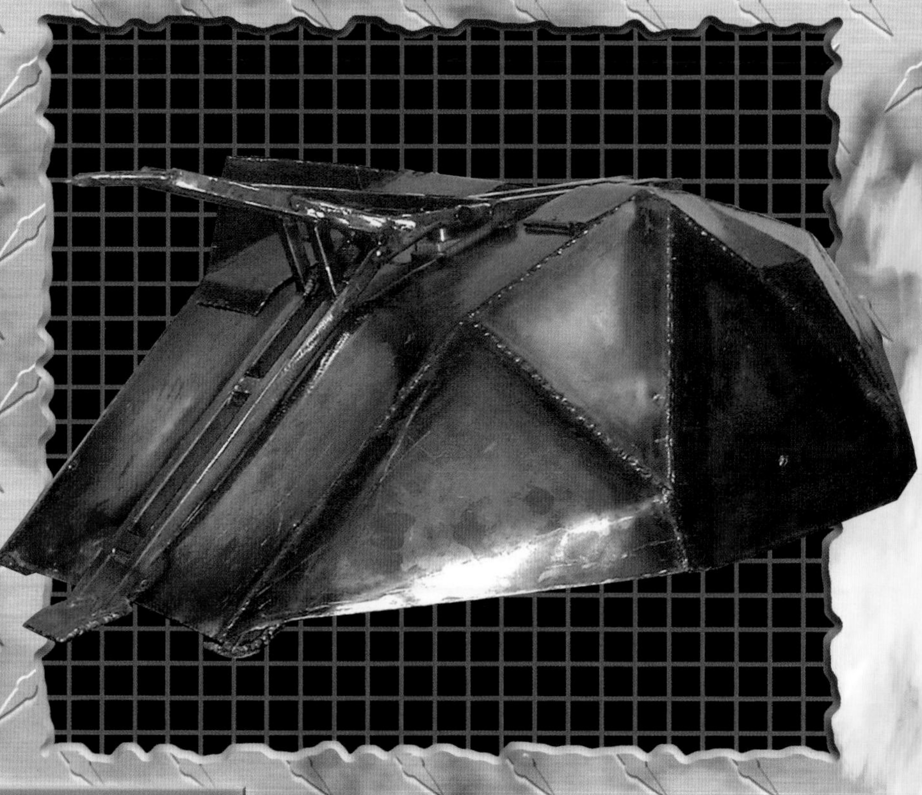

Weight	77.3kg
Dimensions	0.9m x 0.9m x 0.3m
Speed	10mph
Turning Circle	0m
Clearance	0mm
Power	2 monster truck windscreen-wiper motors. 4 x batteries
Weapons	Fierce flipper
Notes	Mild steel shell. Other components include a fire extinguisher and electronic brain
Previous Form	Series 3: won heat final. Knocked out by Mace II in 1st round of semi-finals.
Team	Joseph Watts (captain) and Ian Watts

CLAWED HOPPER

NORTH DEVON

WEIGHT	138.8KG
DIMENSIONS	1.3M X 0.6M X 0.5M
SPEED	3MPH
TURNING CIRCLE	0M
CLEARANCE	N/A – THIS IS A WALKING ROBOT
POWER	3 STARTER MOTORS
WEAPONS	2 MECHANICAL CLAWS
NOTES	SOME PARTS CAME FROM THE LOCAL SCRAP HEAP. MADE FROM STEEL AND ALUMINIUM
PREVIOUS FORM	FIRST-TIME COMPETITORS
TEAM	ANDREW HUGHES (CAPTAIN), NICHOLAS CLEMENT AND JOSHUA HUGHES

Hammer & Tong

Wragby, Lincolnshire

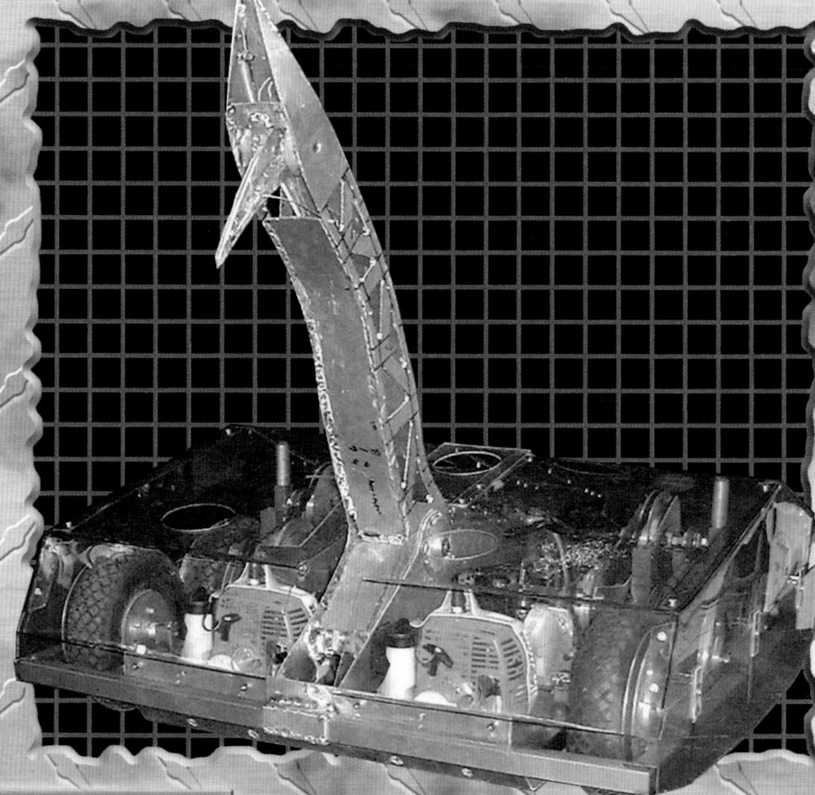

Weight	79.8kg
Dimensions	1m x 1m x 0.7m
Speed	7mph
Turning Circle	0m
Clearance	20mm
Power	2 strimmer motors with petrol engines
Weapons	Pneumatic arm with spike
Notes	Scavenged the flipper from a mate
Previous Form	First-time competitors
Team	Stewart Smith (captain), Oliver Smith and Paul Schmidt

Spikeasaurus

Chorley, nr Preston

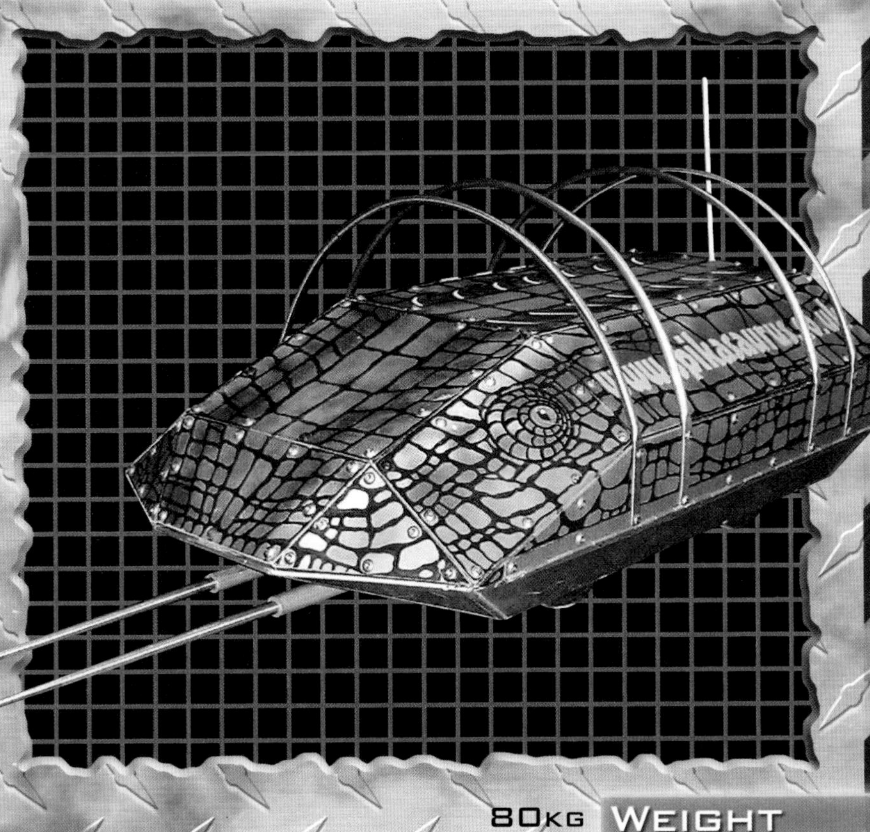

80kg	Weight
1.45m x 0.65m x 0.33m	Dimensions
Up to 17mph	Speed
0m	Turning Circle
42mm	Clearance
4 x 750-watt Bosch motors. Could pull a car	Power
2 x 45cm steel spikes at front with interchangeable ramming bar	Weapons
Self-righting mechanism	Notes
First-time competitors	Previous Form
Stuart Pearson (captain), Andrea Whittle and Lee Ainscough	Team

Bulldog Breed 2

Walsall

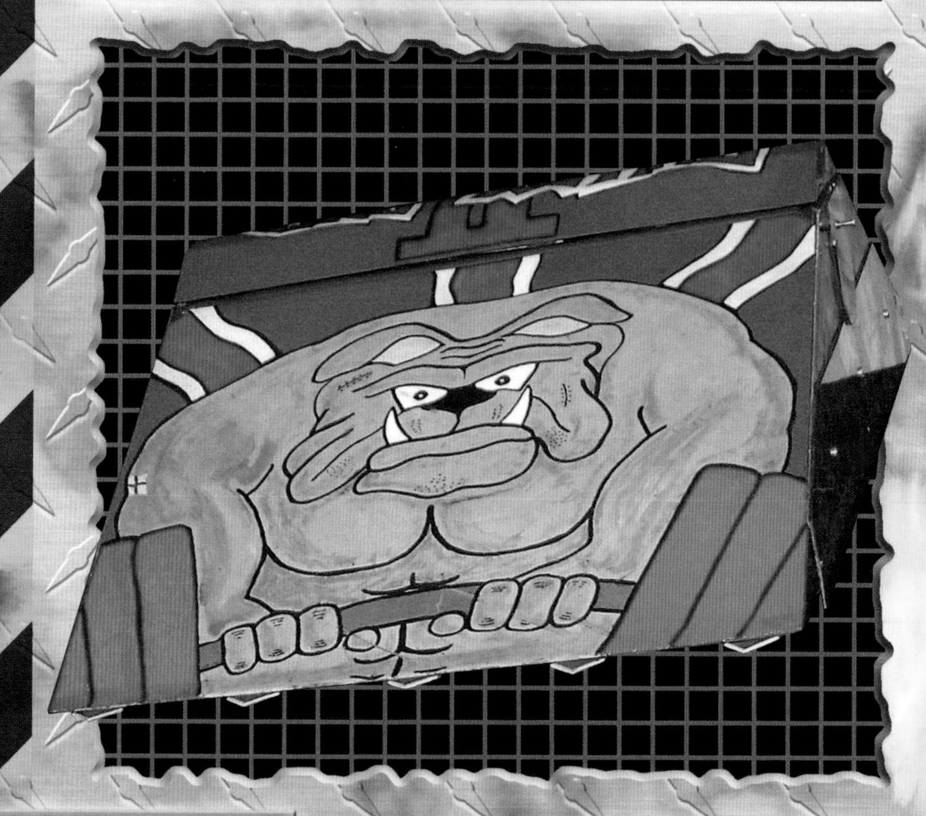

Weight	79.7kg
Dimensions	0.75m x 0.7m x 0.3m
Speed	7mph
Turning Circle	0m
Clearance	15mm
Power	2 wheelchair motors
Weapons	Flipper and rear spike
Notes	Shell is 3mm steel, polycarbonate, aluminium and titanium. Total cost £165. Can push a 2-tonne forklift. When tested, the flipper threw 2 men 2.5m into the air!
Previous Form	Series 3: knocked out by RoboPig in 1st round of heats
Team	Tony Somerfield (captain), Robert Somerfield and Toni Bond

(seed 30) Stinger

Lincoln

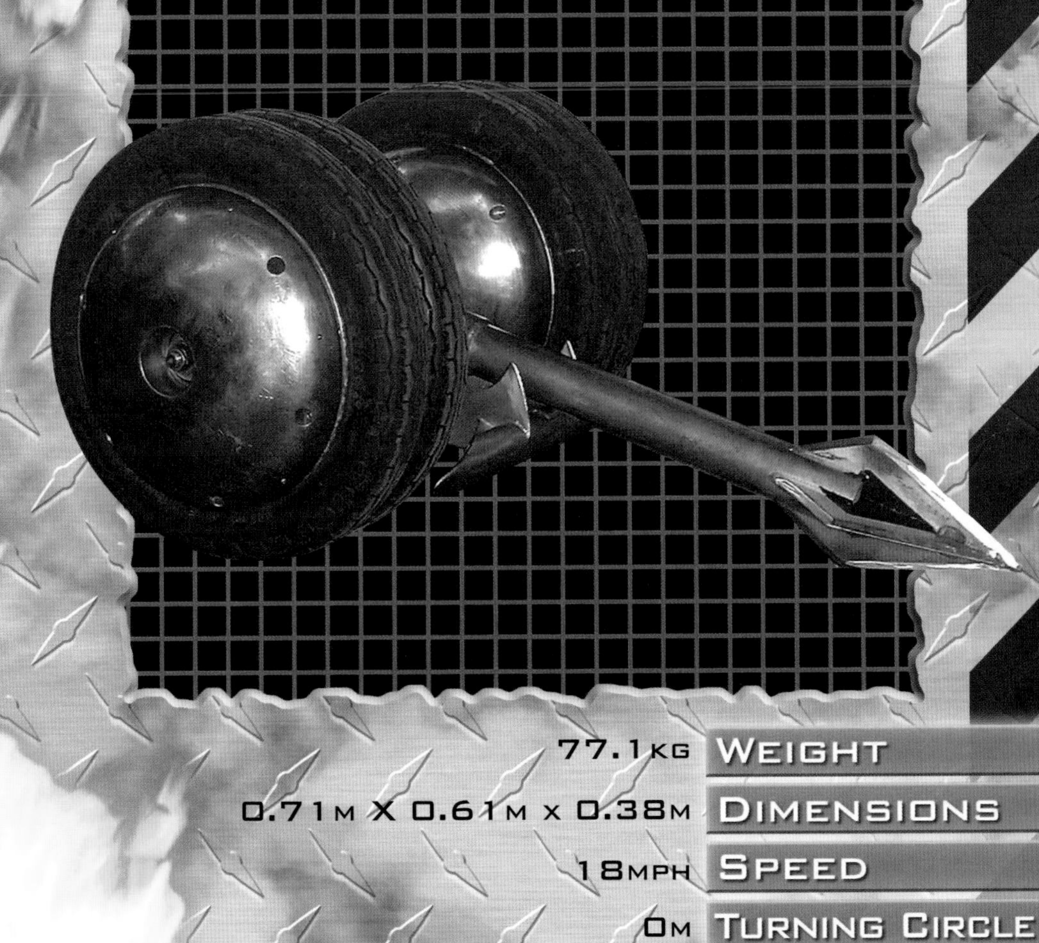

77.1kg	Weight
0.71m X 0.61m x 0.38m	Dimensions
18mph	Speed
0m	Turning Circle
50mm	Clearance
2 x 750-watt Bosch motors	Power
Narrow shaped axe on back	Weapons
Steel shell. All motors, power electronics, receivers and batteries are mounted in the wheels	Notes
Series 3: knocked out by Mace 2 in 1st round of heats	Previous Form
Kevin Scott (captain), Karl Skinner and Tim Mann	Team

Battle Board
Heat K

MouseTrap

Evil Weevil — Tiberius

Sumpthing

Wel'dor — Little Fly

Heat L

Spawn of Scutter

Knightmare — Banshee

Vercingetorix

Fat Boy Tin — Plunderbird 4

Eliminator

MouseTrap

Oxford and Bristol

77.3kg	Weight
1.4m x 0.7m x 0.25m	Dimensions
12.5mph	Speed
0m	Turning Circle
20mm	Clearance
2 x 24v motors	Power
Mousetrap weapon powered by CO_2	Weapons
Made from steel and Lexan. The chassis used to be an office desk. Many parts came from scrapyards	Notes
Series 3 (as Tri-Terra-Bot): knocked out by Evil Weevil in 1st round of heats	Previous Form
Stan Launchbury (captain) and Jason Launchbury	Team

Evil Weevil

Cardiff (seed 12)

Weight	80.2kg
Dimensions	1.1m x 0.7m x 0.3m
Speed	10mph
Turning Circle	1m
Clearance	20mm
Power	2 Sinclair-C5 motors
Weapons	Spikes, a pneumatic sledge hammer
Notes	Shell is a fibreglass/Kevlar mix. Powered by a Sodastream bottle. The base is from a Securicor van
Previous Form	Series 3: won heat final. Knocked out by Hypno-Disc in 1st round of semi-final
Team	Kevin Pritchard (captain), Ashley Evans and Mark Mellor

Tiberius

Brighton

79.9kg	Weight
1.12m x 0.81m x 0.7m	Dimensions
8mph	Speed
0m	Turning Circle
8mm	Clearance
2 x 750-watt motors	Power
Armour piercer made of steel, powered by a car jack	Weapons
Welded steel chassis, armour is polyproplene, Lexan, nylon and steel. Gear from a Honda motorbike	Notes
First-time competitors	Previous Form
Sam Smith (captain), Simon Coulthard and John Coulthard	Team

Sumpthing
Leicestershire

Weight	79.6kg
Dimensions	1.04m x 0.95m x 0.51m
Speed	20mph
Turning Circle	0m
Clearance	8mm
Power	4 starter motors
Weapons	Pickaxe, ramming spikes, wedge
Notes	Most parts have been scavenged from skips. Built over 2 years
Previous Form	Series 3: knocked out by Pit Bull in 1st round of heats
Team	Richard Dig (captain), Jon Lort and Geoff Germainey

Wel'dor

(seed 28) Belfast

80.4kg	Weight
1.2m x 0.95m x 0.35m	Dimensions
14mph	Speed
0m	Turning Circle
0–80mm gradient	Clearance
2 x 750-watt Bosch motors	Power
Pneumatic hammer. A self-righting ram that can flip robots	Weapons
6mm polycarbonate shell and aluminium chassis. 2 go-kart wheels	Notes
Series 3: knocked out by King Buxton in 2nd round of heat	Previous Form
Phelim Lundy (captain), Damian Kilgallon and David Lundy	Team

Little Fly

Langdon, nr Dover

Weight	79.8kg
Dimensions	1.2m x 0.9m x 0.5m
Speed	4mph
Turning Circle	0m
Clearance	50mm
Power	2 wheelchair motors and 1 lawnmower motor
Weapons	Agricultural lawnmower blade
Notes	2 go-kart wheels. Aluminium shell
Previous Form	First-time competitors

Team Andy Hosking (captain), John Woodward and Richard Woodward

Spawn of Scutter

(seed 10) Essex

78.8kg	Weight
1.25m x 1.15m x 0.3m	Dimensions
15mph	Speed
0m	Turning Circle
10mm	Clearance
2 starter motors from a Granada	Power
Pneumatic flipping piercing spike. Pivoting defence ram	Weapons
Wheels from a sack barrow. Shell is 3mm polycarbonate. Runs both ways up	Notes
Series 3 (as Scutter's Revenge): knocked out by 101 in semi-finals	Previous Form
Darren Ball (captain), Graham Warner and Luke Jackman	Team

KNIGHTMARE

LEICESTER

WEIGHT	79.7KG
DIMENSIONS	0.7M X 0.115M X 0.45M
SPEED	10MPH
TURNING CIRCLE	0M
CLEARANCE	20MM
POWER	2X 750-WATT, 24V MOTORS
WEAPONS	PNEUMATIC FLIPPER, SELF-RIGHTING
NOTES	DRIVES BOTH WAYS UP. PANELS ARE MADE FROM MOTORWAY SIGNS. TOOK 12 WEEKS TO MAKE
PREVIOUS FORM	FIRST-TIME COMPETITORS

TEAM	NIGEL PAGET (CAPTAIN), MALCOLM SUMMERS AND LEE SUMMERS

Banshee

Huddersfield

80.3kg	Weight
1m x 1m x 0.9m	Dimensions
5mph	Speed
0m	Turning Circle
10mm	Clearance
2 x 12v batteries for drive 1 x 12v battery for weapon	Power
Made from 4 lathe tools	Weapons
This robot revolves! Took less than 5 weeks to build	Notes
Series 3 (as Shark Attack): knocked out by Behemoth in 1st round of heats	Previous Form
Graham Walker (captain), Richard Jackson and Alan Marchington	Team

Vercingetorix

Isle of Wight

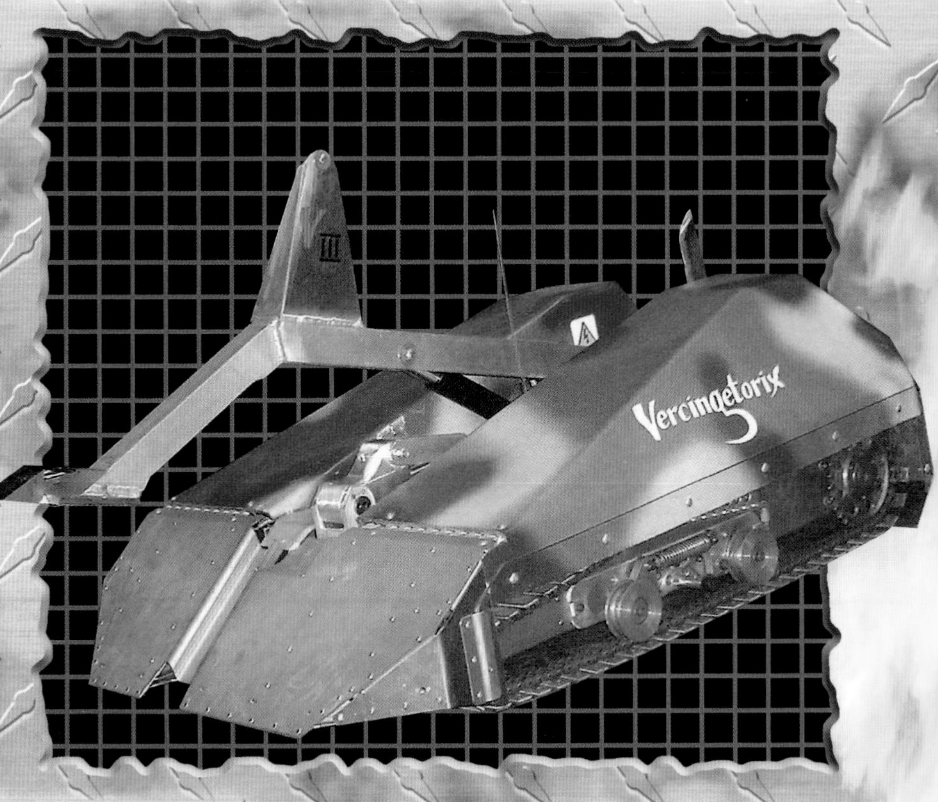

Weight	80.1kg
Dimensions	1.14m x 0.81m x 0.33m
Speed	6mph
Turning Circle	0m
Clearance	2mm
Power	4 x 750-watt motors
Weapons	Axe and lifter
Notes	Made of Kevlar and Lexan
Previous Form	Series 2: knocked out by Haardvark in heats. Series 3: knocked out by Terrorpin in 1st round of heats
Team	Ian Gear (captain), Tom Curtis-Horsfall and Alistair Curtis-Horsfall

Fat Boy Tin

Leighton Buzzard

77.1kg	Weight
0.9m x 0.8m x 1.2m	Dimensions
15mph	Speed
0m	Turning Circle
15mm	Clearance
1 x 24v wheelchair motor 2 x 12v wiper motors	Power
2 pneumatic spikes	Weapons
Chassis is steel, rest of robot is aluminium. Built for under £200	Notes
First-time competitors	Previous Form
John Lewis (captain) and Richard Lewis	Team

Plunderbird 4

Hampshire (seed 26)

Weight	80.3kg
Dimensions	0.94m x 0.66m x 0.41m
Speed	15mph
Turning Circle	0m
Clearance	2mm
Power	2 x 24v 160-watt motors
Weapons	Main weapons are fear, surprise and brute force. Also has a slicer dicer
Notes	Shell is aeroplane-standard aluminium. Tracked
Previous Form	Series 1: knocked out in 1st round of heats. Series 2: knocked out in first round of semi-final. Series 3: lost to Thermidor in 1st round of heats due to a technical malfunction
Team	Mike Onslow (captain) and Bryan Kilburn

Battle Board

Heat M

The Steel Avenger

Wild Thing

Humphrey

Sir Chromalot

Scorpion

Reactor

Heat N

Arnold, Arnold Terminegger

Behemoth

Rambot

X-terminator II

Judge Shred II

Millennium Bug

Eliminator

Steel Avenger

Suffolk

Weight	79.6kg
Dimensions	1.22m x 0.65m x 0.71m
Speed	15mph
Turning Circle	0m
Clearance	50mm
Power	2 x 750-watt Bosch motors
Weapons	Pneumatically powered axe
Notes	Shell made from aluminium, steel and polycarbonate
Previous Form	Series 3: knocked out by Diótóir in 2nd round of heats

Team John Willoughby (captain), Kevin Cockerill and Tony Bates

Humphrey

Lincoln

79.8kg	Weight
1.3m x 1.1m x 0.3m	Dimensions
6mph	Speed
0m	Turning Circle
5mm	Clearance
3 x 24v motors	Power
Lifting arm made from a car jack. Spikes	Weapons
The sproggets for the gearbox are from 3 lawnmowers. There's an old table leg in there somewhere!	Notes
First-time competitors	Previous Form
Mick Kerfoot (captain), Helen Kerfoot and Robert Holmes	Team

Wild Thing (seed 11)

Hampshire

Weight	76.4kg
Dimensions	0.79m x 0.92m x 0.46m
Speed	8mph
Turning Circle	0m
Clearance	0mm
Power	2 x industrial electric motors
Weapons	Multi-purpose – lifter arm/lance to stab/self-righting mechanism
Notes	Aluminium shell. 2 go-kart wheels. 2 x 50-watt bulbs for the eyes
Previous Form	Series 3 (as Thing): won heat final. Knocked out by Panic Attack in 1st round of semi-final
Team	Nick Adams (captain), Isabelle Adams and Jake Adams

Sir Chromalot

(seed 27) Shropshire

80.3kg	Weight
0.61m diameter x 0.41m	Dimensions
10mph	Speed
0m	Turning Circle
0mm	Clearance
4 industrial-drill motors	Power
45cm rotating drill, stainless steel cone with 2 cobalt cutters	Weapons
Shell is a 25mm American truck wheel hub. Insides protected by a fireblanket. Self-righting	Notes
Series 3: knocked out by Big Brother in 2nd round of heats	Previous Form
Steve Merrill (captain) and Dave Whitehead	Team

Scorpion

Farnham, Surrey/Nutley, E.Sussex

Weight	76.2kg
Dimensions	1.4m x 0.7m x 0.8m
Speed	7mph
Turning Circle	0m
Clearance	50mm
Power	2 wheelchair motors
Weapons	2 electrically powered chainsaw cutting discs
Notes	The team used an old tumble dryer to practise on as an opponent
Previous Form	First-time competitors
Team	Geoff Smith (captain) and John Bell

Reactor

Leicester

80.2kg	Weight
1.3m x 0.8m x 0.8m	Dimensions
10–12mph	Speed
0m	Turning Circle
5mm	Clearance
2 wheelchair motors	Power
Front flipper. Self-righting mechanism	Weapons
Steel and aluminium shell. Custom-built wheels made from wood, steel and rubber	Notes
First-time competitors	Previous Form

Russell Orton (captain), Daniel Orton and Martin Crouch **Team**

Arnold, Arnold Terminegger
High Wycombe

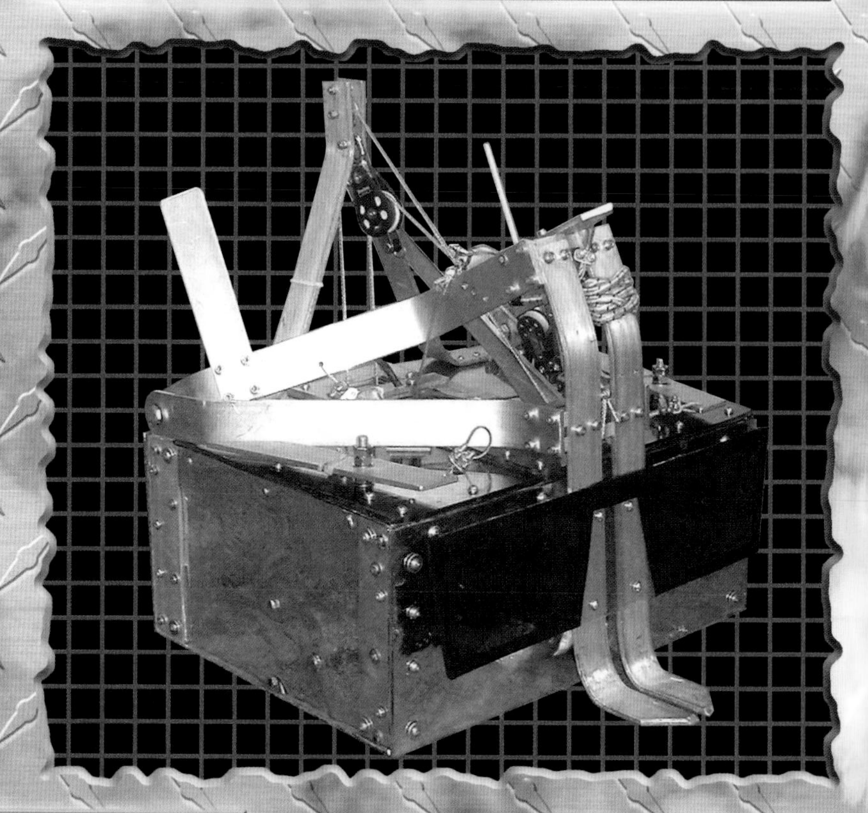

Weight	73.6kg
Dimensions	0.45m x 0.8m x 0.6m
Speed	5–8mph
Turning Circle	0m
Clearance	19mm
Power	2 x 750-watt Bosch motors
Weapons	Lifter
Notes	The chassis is from a cold-water storage tank. Also includes parts from a boat. Self-righting
Previous Form	Series 3 (as Miss Struts): beat Stomp to win the Walker competition
Team	Ian Inglis (captain), William Inglis and Holly Inglis

(seed 6) Behemoth

Hemel Hempstead

80.4kg	Weight
1.1m x 0.62m x 0.57m	Dimensions
6mph	Speed
0m	Turning Circle
25mm	Clearance
2 x 750-watt Bosch motors that lead into a wheelchair gearbox	Power
Pneumatic scoop	Weapons
Titanium shell. 5mm titanium on the bucket	Notes
Series 2: won heat final. Lost to Killertron in semi-final. Series 3: flipped by arena spike in heat final against Pit Bull	Previous Form
Anthony Pritchard (captain), Michael Pritchard and Kane Aston	Team

RAMBOT

POTTERS BAR

WEIGHT	79KG
DIMENSIONS	1.2M x 0.6M x 0.25M
SPEED	20MPH
TURNING CIRCLE	0.6M
CLEARANCE	10MM
POWER	2 x 750-WATT BOSCH MOTORS; 240-WATT BATTERIES
WEAPONS	2 STEEL SPIKES ON BACK AND 2 ON FRONT – ACT AS LIFTING DEVICES
NOTES	ALUMINIUM SHELL WITH STEEL TUBING INSIDE. TITANIUM INNER SHELL FOR PROTECTION. TOOK 7 MONTHS TO BUILD
PREVIOUS FORM	FIRST-TIME COMPETITORS

TEAM DAVID JOHNSON (CAPTAIN), TIM DENYER AND MUHUNTHAN THANGESWARAN

X-terminator II

(seed 22) Hereford

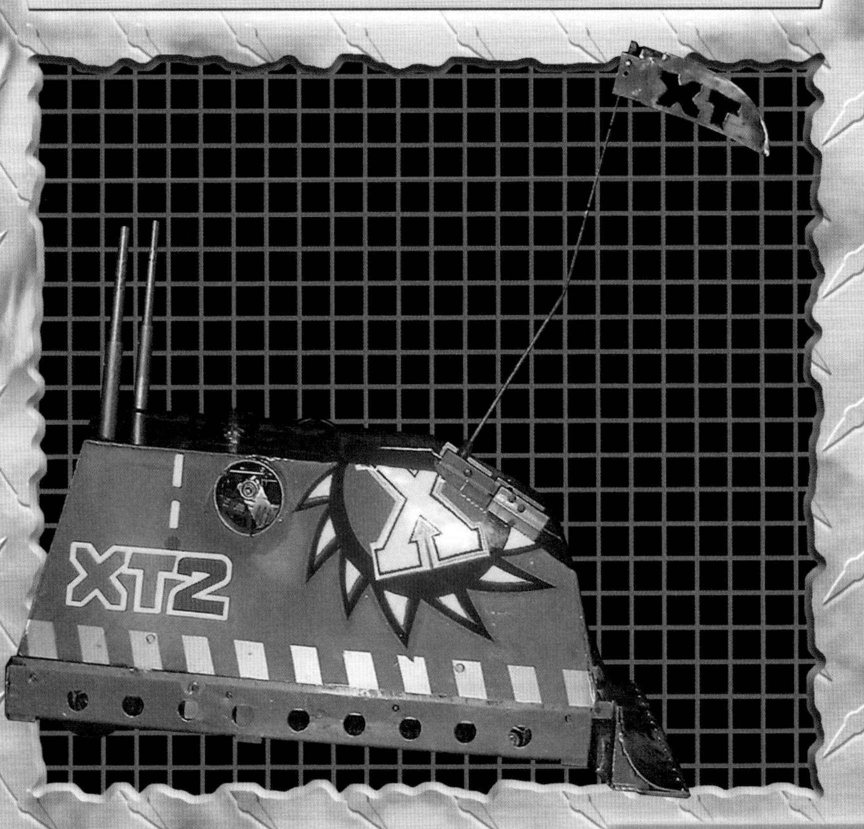

80.1kg	Weight
0.8m x 0.6m x 0.5m	Dimensions
25mph	Speed
0m	Turning Circle
15mm	Clearance
2 x 750-watt Bosch motors	Power
Interchangeable axe or flipper. Scoop bucket	Weapons
Aluminium shell	Notes
Series 3: knocked out by Panic Attack in the heat final	Previous Form
Marlon Pritchard (captain), Paul Lewis and Simon Baldwin	Team

Judge Shred II

Leicester

Weight	80.5kg
Dimensions	0.91m x 0.76m x 0.20m
Speed	7mph
Turning Circle	0.60m
Clearance	10mm
Power	4 wheelchair motors
Weapons	Pneumatic axe and a wedge to flip. Self-righting
Notes	Shell made of polycarbonate and alloy. Other materials were begged, stolen or borrowed
Previous Form	Series 3: knocked into the pit by X-terminator in 2nd round of heats

Team Alan Blakeman (captain), Paul Blakeman and Dave Cluley

Millennium Bug

Norwich

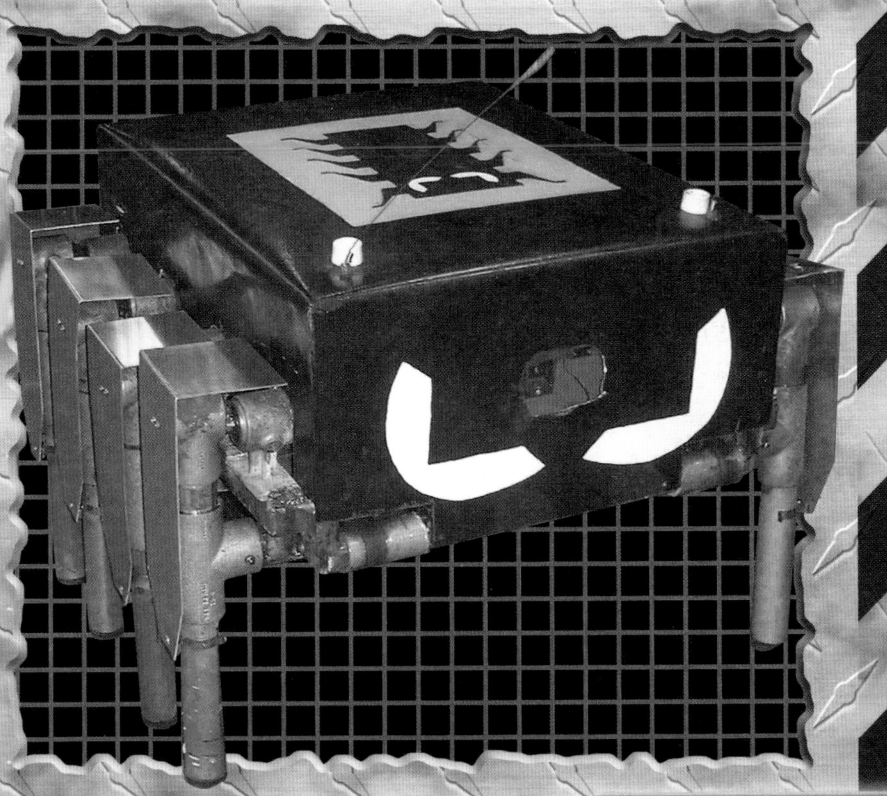

160kg	Weight
0.72m x 0.65m x 0.45m	Dimensions
4mph	Speed
0m	Turning Circle
250mm	Clearance
2 disabled-scooter motors	Power
Disc rotating at 2,000rpm	Weapons
The legs are scaffold pipes. The shell is 3mm steel	Notes
First-time competitors	Previous Form
Rory Williams (captain), Thomas Williams and Andrew Walker	Team

Battle Board
Heat O

S.M.I.D.S.Y.

Panic Attack II | Overkill GTI

Aggrobot II

Oblivion II | Sawpoint

Heat P

The Predator

Hypno-Disc | Raizer Blade

Cerberus

Onslaught | Terror-Bull

Eliminator

S.M.I.D.S.Y.*

Kent, Sussex and Yorkshire (team formed over internet)

78kg	Weight
1.22m x 0.61m x 0.30m	Dimensions
10mph	Speed
0m	Turning Circle
25mm (adjustable)	Clearance
2 x 750-watt Bosch motors	Power
Spikes and jaws	Weapons
Shell of steel, plastic and titanium. Jaws operated by Jaguar seat actuators. 4 go-kart wheels. Runs upside down	Notes
Series 3: lost to Rattus Rattus in 2nd round of heats due to radio signal problems	Previous Form
Mik Reed (captain), Robin Bennett and Andy Pugh	Team

*Sorry mate I didn't see you

Panic Attack II

Cwmbran (seed 4)

Weight	80.6kg
Dimensions	1m x 0.7m x 0.16m
Speed	7mph
Turning Circle	0m
Clearance	0mm
Power	2 lorry windscreen-wiper motors
Weapons	Electric lifting forks
Notes	Shell is aluminium, polycarbonate and bulletproof fibreglass
Previous Form	Series 2: won heat and semi-final. Beat Cassius to become Grand Champion. Series 3: knocked out by Fire Storm in 2nd round of semi-final
Team	Kim Davies (captain), Michael Davies and Christian Bridge

Overkill GTI

Weston super Mare

77.8kg	Weight
1.2m x 0.8m x 0.45m	Dimensions
10mph	Speed
0m	Turning Circle
(Adjustable) 0 to 100mm	Clearance
2 caravan winch motors	Power
2 pneumatic flipper arms	Weapons
Polycarbonate and steel body. Motors have been rewound with Teflon and Nomex insulation (used for space travel) so they are fireproof	Notes
Series 3: knocked out by 101 in 1st round of heat	Previous Form
Lawrence Burke (captain), Lawrie Burke and James Yule	Team

AGGROBOT II (SEED 20)

DORKING

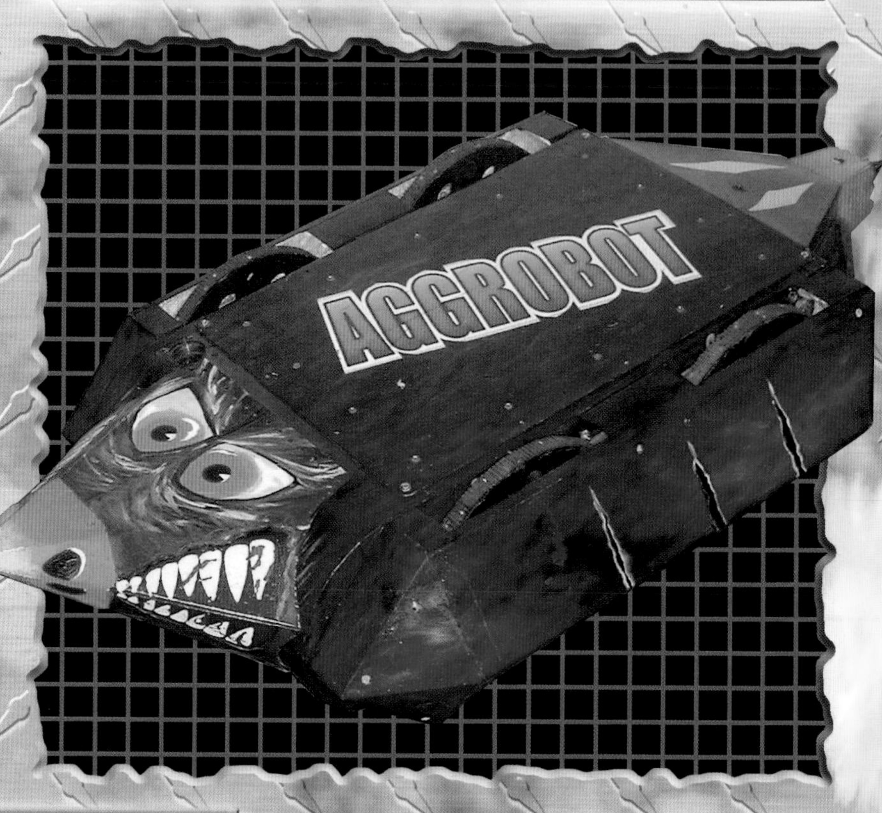

WEIGHT	79.7KG
DIMENSIONS	1.7M X 0.87M X 0.35M
SPEED	6MPH
TURNING CIRCLE	0M
CLEARANCE	40MM
POWER	2 ELECTRIC-WHEELCHAIR MOTORS
WEAPONS	HYDRAULIC ZONKER – A CAPTIVE CROSSBOW. LIFTING NOSE CONE
NOTES	SHELL IS ALUMINIUM ALLOY OBTAINED FROM A SKIP. WHEELS ARE CUSTOM-BUILT
PREVIOUS FORM	SERIES 3 (AS AGGROBOT): KNOCKED OUT BY BLADE IN HEAT FINAL
TEAM	PETER LEACH (CAPTAIN), BOB LEACH AND JOHN LEACH

Oblivion II

Wallington, Surrey

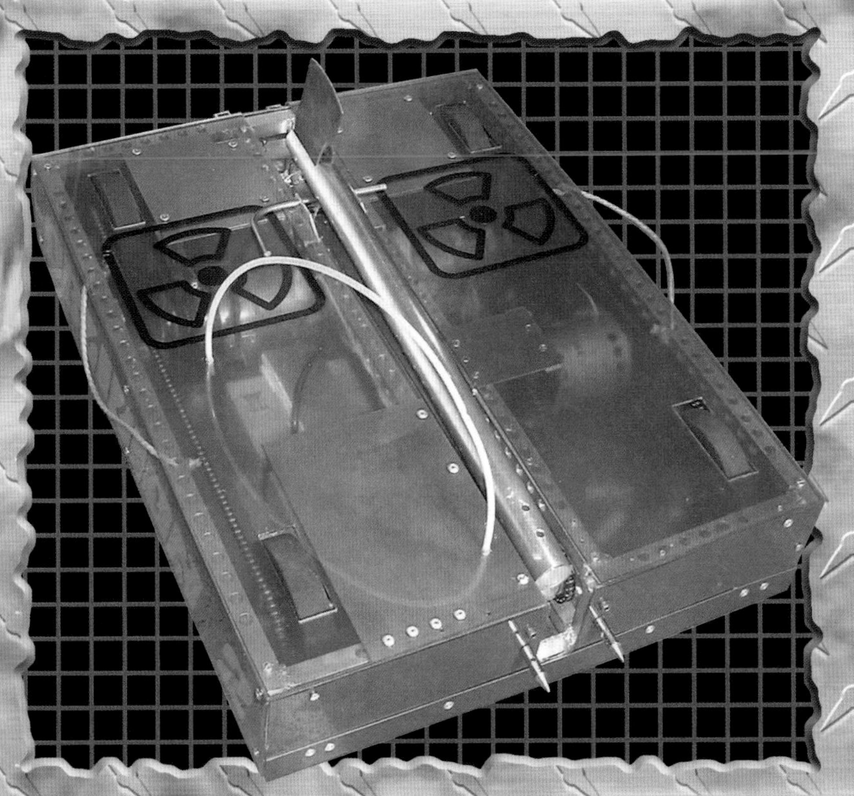

79.5kg	Weight
1m x 0.75m x 0.2m	Dimensions
10mph	Speed
0m	Turning Circle
0mm	Clearance
Drive motors from a Sinclair C5	Power
Electric axe	Weapons
Made from titanium dural and polycarbonate. Armour is aerospace-grade	Notes
Series 2 (as Oblivion): knocked out by Mortis in heat final. Series 3: competed in Pinball competiton	Previous Form
Suren Balendran (captain), Thuvaaragan and Suppiah Balendran	Team

Sawpoint

Burnham-on-Crouch, Essex

Weight	79.3kg
Dimensions	1.2m x 0.45m x 0.6m
Speed	8mph
Turning Circle	0m
Clearance	100mm
Power	2 x 24v wheelchair motors
Weapons	Motorized ramming spike. Saw blades. Moveable snow plough
Notes	Made from mild steel sheet/ polycarbonate sheet. The prototype was made from Meccano
Previous Form	First-time competitors

Team Stephen Thomas (captain) and Damien Smith

The Predator

Manchester

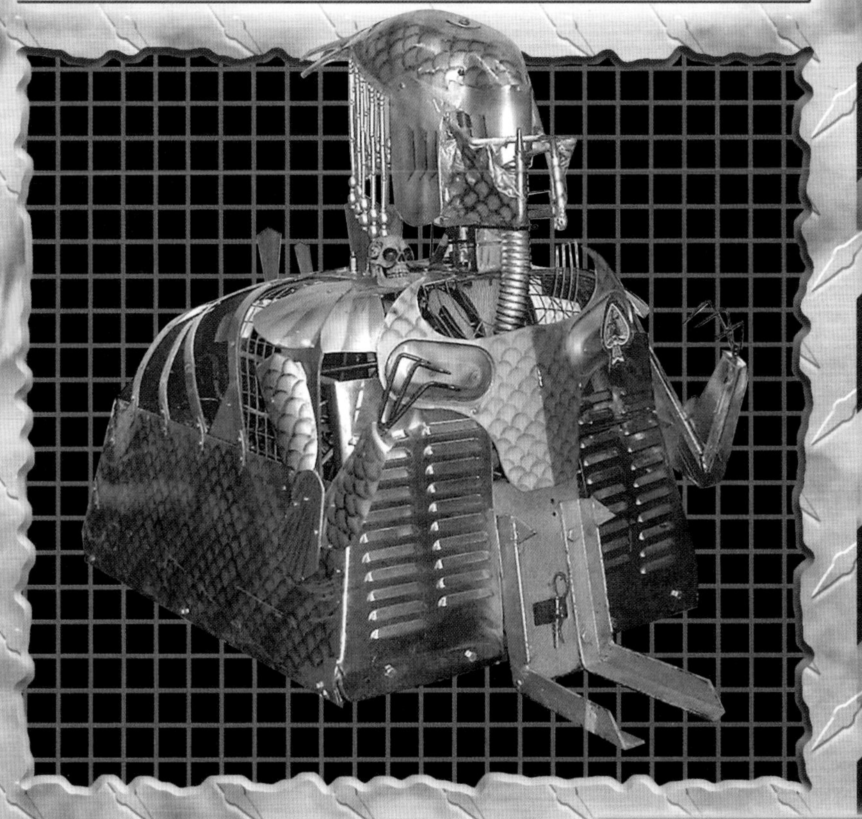

78.6kg	Weight
1.3m x 0.75m x 1m	Dimensions
8mph	Speed
0m	Turning Circle
15mm	Clearance
2 wheelchair motors	Power
Pneumatic front-lifting fork and rear spike pickaxe	Weapons
Made from aluminium-covered Teflon. The head is a wok, the dreadlocks are a beaded curtain. Chassis made from police van armour plating	Notes
Series 3 (as Crippler): knocked out by All Torque in 1st round of heat	Previous Form
Barry Willetts (captain), Christopher Willetts and Stephen Willetts	Team

Hypno-Disc (seed 2)

Banbury

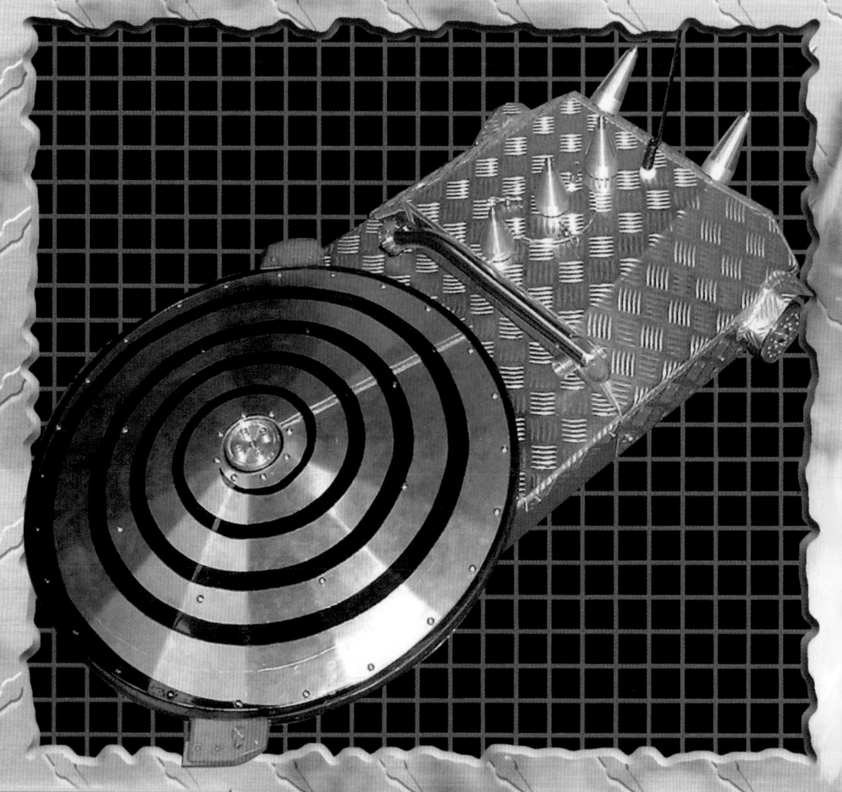

Weight	80.6kg
Dimensions	0.91m x 0.56m x 0.25m
Speed	20mph
Turning Circle	0m
Clearance	40mm
Power	3 x 750-watt, 24v motors
Weapons	Disk spinning at 750rpm
Notes	Aluminium and mild steel shell. Custom-made wheels
Previous Form	Series 3: Beat Beserk II to win heat final. Beat 101 to win semi-final. Knocked out Steg-O-Saw-Us in 1st round of final but lost to Chaos 2 in Grand Final
Team	Dave Rose (captain), Derek Rose and Ken Rose

RAIZER BLADE

CAMBRIDGE

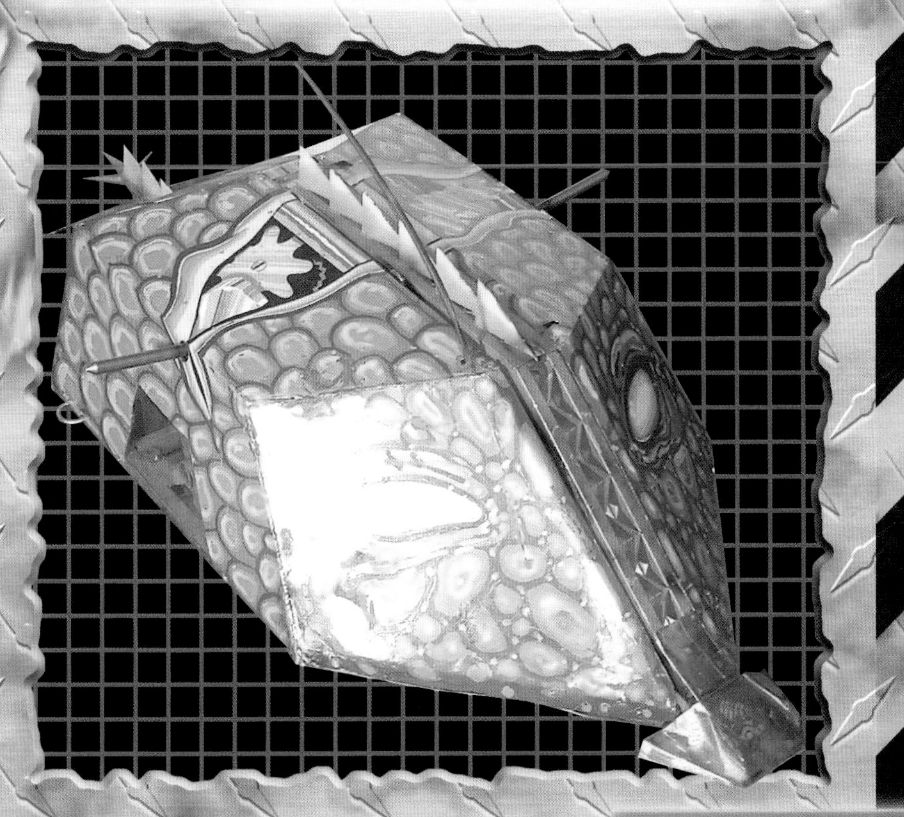

79.2KG	WEIGHT
1.5M X 0.75M X 0.5M	DIMENSIONS
12MPH	SPEED
0M	TURNING CIRCLE
2–50MM GRADIENT	CLEARANCE
2 X 750-WATT, 24V MOTORS	POWER
HYDRAULIC LIFT AND SPIKE	WEAPONS
HYDRAULICS FROM A FORD GRANADA BRAKING SYSTEM. MADE FROM ALUMINIUM AND STEEL	NOTES
SERIES 3: KNOCKED OUT BY SUICIDAL TENDENCIES IN 2ND ROUND OF HEATS	PREVIOUS FORM
PAUL HART (CAPTAIN), STEVE SCOTCHER AND HOWARD ANDREWS	TEAM

Cerberus (seed 18)

London

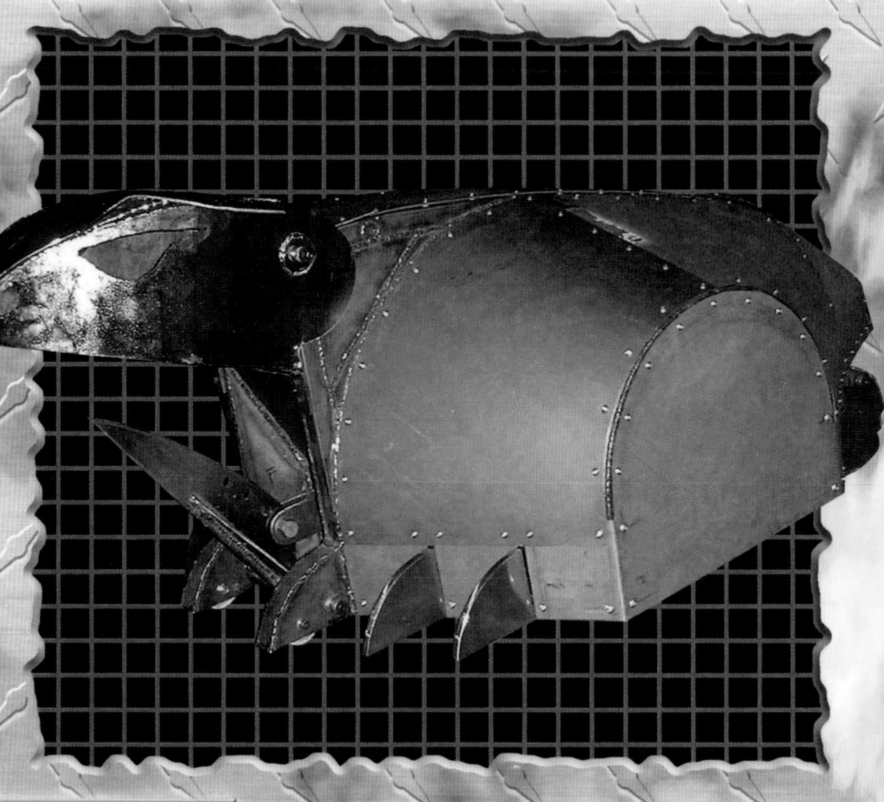

Weight	80kg
Dimensions	0.7m x 0.76m x 0.45m
Speed	16mph
Turning Circle	0m
Clearance	20mm
Power	2 x 750-watt, 24v motors
Weapons	Fixed steel claws, a mouth for eating other robots!
Notes	Built in 8 weeks for £350. Body made of scrap titanium
Previous Form	Series 3: knocked out by Thing in heat final

Team Theo Kaccoufa (captain), Vassile Kaccoufa and Alex Wink

ONSLAUGHT

BEDFORD

80.2KG	WEIGHT
1M x 0.6M x 0.6M	DIMENSIONS
12MPH	SPEED
2M	TURNING CIRCLE
5MM	CLEARANCE
FORKLIFT TRUCK ELECTRIC MOTOR	POWER
PNEUMATICALLY POWERED SCOOPER. STATIC SPIKES AT REAR	WEAPONS
SELF-RIGHTING MECHANISM. STEEL CHASSIS	NOTES
SERIES 3: KNOCKED OUT BY THE BEAST OF BODMIN IN 2ND ROUND OF HEAT	PREVIOUS FORM
ALAN WOOD (CAPTAIN), DAVID WOOD AND MARK HOLLAND	TEAM

Terror-Bull

Ilkley, West Yorkshire

Weight	80.4kg
Dimensions	0.91m x 0.61m x 0.36m
Speed	30mph
Turning Circle	0m
Clearance	25mm
Power	2 x 750-watt, 24v motors
Weapons	2 spikes in the head and tongue – the entire head is pneumatic
Notes	3mm aluminium shell on a box section chassis
Previous Form	First-time competitors

Team John Fearnley (captain) and Ben Fearnley

Robot Wars Terminology

Roboteers/Robot Warriors – generic term for individuals who create and operate robots

Drivers – specific term for those individuals who control robots

Trials – games and challenges designed to test robots who want to compete in the wars

Arena – enclosed area in which combat takes place, alternatively known as the 'combat arena' or the 'battle zone'

Pits (The) – backstage workshops and staging area for all Robot Wars events and television recordings

Test Area – separate area for the testing of robots before competition or combat

Weigh-in area – where robots are weighed, measured and processed

Transmitter Control – area set aside for the control and policing of transmitters during the event/recording

Pits Marshalls – officials who police the pits area and ensure Health and Safetly policies are being implemented fully

Weight Category – weight classification of robot as specified in the rules and regulations, categories include Featherweight, Lightweight, Middleweight, Heavyweight and Super Heavyweight

Face-offs – a two-robot battle

Melees – a battle featuring three or more robots

Grudge Match – a battle featuring two or more robots to settle a disagreement or grudge

Excessive Evasion – term used to describe the cowardly behaviour of a robot that won't fight for fear of getting destroyed

House Robots – the shows own super-robots, named Matilda, Dead Metal, Shunt, Sergeant Bash, Sir Killalot and RefBot

INDEX